# Financial & Managerial Accounting

## FOURTEENTH EDITION

### Carl S. Warren
Professor Emeritus of Accounting
University of Georgia, Athens

### James M. Reeve
Professor Emeritus of Accounting
University of Tennessee, Knoxville

### Jonathan E. Duchac
Professor of Accounting
Wake Forest University

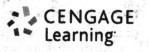

CENGAGE
Learning

Australia • Brazil • Mexico • Singapore • United Kingdom • United States

For product information and technology assistance, contact us at **Cengage Learning Academic Resource Center, 1-800-423-0563**.

For permission to use material from this text or product, submit all requests online at **www.cengage.com/permissions**. Further permissions questions can be emailed to **permissionrequest@cengage.com**.

ISBN: 978-1-337-27062-5

**Cengage Learning**
20 Channel Center Street
Boston, MA 02210
USA

Cengage Learning is a leading provider of customized learning solutions with employees residing in nearly 40 different countries and sales in more than 125 countries around the world. Find your local representative at **www.cengage.com**.

Cengage Learning products are represented in Canada by Nelson Education, Ltd.

To learn more about Cengage Learning Solutions, visit **www.cengage.com**.

Purchase any of our products at your local college store or at our preferred online store **www.cengagebrain.com**.

Printed in the United States of America
Print Number: 01     Print Year: 2016

# CONTENTS

The working papers include problem-specific forms for preparing solutions for Exercises, A&B Problems, the Continuing Problem, and the Comprehensive Problems from the textbook. These forms, with preprinted headings, provide a structure for the problems, which will help you get started and save you time.

Based on students' testimonials and instructors' feedback, the forms in the working papers have been streamlined to make them simpler to use and to better reflect the changing environment of business. For example, the vertical rules that separated digits of numbers entered into journals, ledgers, and statements have been removed, making it easier to write in numbers.

Note that when entering whole amounts into the forms, your instructor will direct you on whether to include a decimal point and zeroes (e.g., 100.00) or to omit those (e.g., 100).

**EXERCISE 15-1**

**A.** Depreciation of robotic assembly line equipment: _____

**B.** V8 automobile engine: _____

**C.** Steering wheel: _____

**D.** Wheels: _____

**E.** Painting safety masks for employees working in the paint room: _____

**F.** Salary of test driver: _____

**G.** Glass used in the vehicle's windshield: _____

**H.** Wages of assembly line worker: _____

**EXERCISE 15-2**

**A.** Plant manager salary for the Iowa City, Iowa, plant: _____

**B.** Maintenance supplies: _____

**C.** Salary of process engineers: _____

**D.** Wages paid to Packaging Department employees in the Bear River City, Utah, paper products plant:

_____

**E.** Scents and fragrances used in making soaps and detergents: _____

**F.** Wages of production line employees at the Pineville, Louisiana, soap and detergent plant: _____

_____

**G.** Depreciation on assembly line in the Mehoopany, Pennsylvania, paper products plant: _____

_____

**H.** Packaging materials: _____

**I.** Resins for body wash products: _____

**J.** Depreciation on the Auburn, Maine, manufacturing plant: _____

**EXERCISE 15-3**

**A.** Plant manager's salary at Buffalo, New York, stamping plant, which manufactures auto and truck

subassemblies: _____

**B.** Depreciation on Flat Rock, Michigan, assembly plant: _____

**C.** Dividends paid to shareholders: _____

**D.** Machine lubricant used to maintain the assembly line at the Louisville, Kentucky, assembly plant:

_____

**E.** Leather to be used on vehicles that have leather interiors: _____

**F.** Depreciation on mechanical robots used on the assembly line: _____

**G.** Consultant fees for a study of production line efficiency: _____

**H.** Dealership sales incentives: _____

**I.** Vice president of human resources's salary: _____

**J.** Property taxes on the Dearborn, Michigan, headquarters building: _____

## EXERCISE 15-4

**A.** Research and development costs: _____

**B.** Depreciation on sewing machines: _____

**C.** Fabric used during production: _____

**D.** Depreciation on office equipment: _____

**E.** Advertising expenses: _____

**F.** Repairs and maintenance costs for sewing machines: _____

**G.** Salary of production quality control supervisor: _____

**H.** Utility costs for office building: _____

**I.** Sales commissions: _____

**J.** Salaries of distribution center personnel: _____

**K.** Wages of sewing machine operators: _____

**L.** Factory janitorial supplies: _____

**M.** Chief financial officer's salary: _____

**N.** Travel costs of media relations employees: _____

**O.** Factory supervisors' salaries: _____

**P.** Oil used to lubricate sewing machines: _____

**Q.** Property taxes on factory building and equipment: _____

## EXERCISE 15-5

**A.** _____

**B.** _____

**C.** _____

**D.** _____

**E.** _____

**F.** _____

**G.** _____

**EXERCISE 15-6**

A. _____

B. _____

C. _____

D. _____

E. _____

F. _____

G. _____


**EXERCISE 15-7**

A. Cost to lease (rent) railroad cars: _____

B. Cost of track and bed (ballast) replacement: _____

C. Diesel fuel costs: _____

D. Cost to lease (rent) train locomotives: _____

E. Depreciation of terminal facilities: _____

F. Maintenance costs of right of way, bridges, and buildings: _____

G. Salaries of dispatching and communications personnel: _____

H. Headquarters information technology support staff salaries: _____

I. Safety training costs: _____

J. Wages of train engineers: _____

K. Wages of switch and classification yard personnel: _____

L. Costs of accident cleanup: _____


**EXERCISE 15-8**

1. Energy Efficiency: _____

   _____

2. Fuel Efficiency: _____

   _____

3. Material Use Efficiency: _____

   _____

4. Waste Efficiency: _____

   _____

**EXERCISE 15-9**

1. _____

   _____

   _____

2. _____

   _____

   _____

   _____

   _____

   _____

*Manufacturing Costs*

|  |  |  |
|---|---|---|
|  |  |  |
|  |  |  |
|  |  |  |
|  |  |  |
|  |  |  |
|  |  |  |
|  |  |  |
|  |  |  |
|  |  |  |
|  |  |  |
|  |  |  |
|  |  |  |
|  |  |  |
|  |  |  |

**EXERCISE 15-10**

**A.**

|  |  | *Income Statement* |  |  |
|--|--|--|--|--|
|  |  |  |  |  |
|  |  |  |  |  |
|  |  |  |  |  |
|  |  |  |  |  |
|  |  |  |  |  |
|  |  |  |  |  |
|  |  |  |  |  |
|  |  |  |  |  |
|  |  |  |  |  |

**B.** Inventory balances on March 31:

Materials: _____

_____

Work in Process: _____

_____

Finished Goods: _____

_____

**EXERCISE 15-11**

|  | | |
|---|---|---|
| *Balance Sheet* | | |
| | | |
| | | |
| | | |
| | | |
| | | |
| | | |
| | | |
| | | |
| | | |
| | | |
| | | |
| | | |
| | | |
| | | |
| | | |
| | | |

**EXERCISE 15-12**

|  | |
|---|---|
| | |
| | |
| | |
| | |
| | |
| | |

**EXERCISE 15-13**

| | | | |
|---|---|---|---|
| Work in process inventory, August 1 | $ 19,660 | $ 41,650 | **(E)** _____ |
| Total manufacturing costs incurred during August | 332,750 | **(C)** _____ | 1,075,000 |
| Total manufacturing costs | **(A)** _____ | $515,770 | $1,240,000 |
| Work in process inventory, August 31 | 23,500 | 54,000 | **(F)** _____ |
| Cost of goods manufactured | **(B)** _____ | **(D)** _____ | $1,068,000 |

**EXERCISE 15-14**

| | | |
|---|---|---|
| | | |
| | | |
| | | |
| | | |
| | | |
| | | |
| | | |
| | | |
| | | |
| | | |
| | | |
| | | |
| | | |
| | | |
| | | |
| | | |

**EXERCISE 15-15**

| | | | |
|---|---|---|---|
| Finished goods inventory, June 1 | $116,600 | $ 38,880 | **(E)** _____ |
| Cost of goods manufactured | 825,900 | **(C)** _____ | 180,000 |
| Cost of finished goods available for sale | **(A)** _____ | $540,000 | $1,100,000 |
| Finished goods inventory, June 30 | 130,000 | 70,000 | **(F)** _____ |
| Cost of goods sold | **(B)** _____ | **(D)** _____ | $ 945,000 |

**EXERCISE 15-16**

**A.**

| | | | |
|---|---|---|---|
| *Statement of Cost of Goods Manufactured* | | | |
| | | | |
| | | | |
| | | | |
| | | | |
| | | | |
| | | | |
| | | | |
| | | | |
| | | | |
| | | | |
| | | | |
| | | | |
| | | | |
| | | | |
| | | | |
| | | | |
| | | | |
| | | | |
| | | | |
| | | | |
| | | | |
| | | | |
| | | | |
| | | | |
| | | | |
| | | | |
| | | | |
| | | | |
| | | | |
| | | | |

**EXERCISE 15-16, Concluded**

**B.**

| | | |
|---|---|---|
| | | |
| | | |
| | | |
| | | |
| | | |
| | | |
| | | |

**EXERCISE 15-17**

**A., B., and C.**

| | | |
|---|---|---|
| | | |
| | | |
| | | |
| | | |
| | | |
| | | |
| | | |
| | | |
| | | |
| | | |
| | | |
| | | |
| | | |
| | | |
| | | |
| | | |
| | | |
| | | |
| | | |
| | | |

**EXERCISE 15-18**

**A. through E.**

| | | |
|---|---|---|
| | | |
| | | |
| | | |
| | | |
| | | |
| | | |
| | | |
| | | |
| | | |
| | | |
| | | |
| | | |
| | | |
| | | |
| | | |
| | | |
| | | |
| | | |
| | | |
| | | |
| | | |
| | | |
| | | |
| | | |

**PROBLEM 15-1 ___**

| Cost | Product Costs | | | Period Costs | |
|---|---|---|---|---|---|
| | Direct Materials Cost | Direct Labor Cost | Factory Overhead Cost | Selling Expense | Administrative Expense |
| A. | | | | | |
| B. | | | | | |
| C. | | | | | |
| D. | | | | | |
| E. | | | | | |
| F. | | | | | |
| G. | | | | | |
| H. | | | | | |
| I. | | | | | |
| J. | | | | | |
| K. | | | | | |
| L. | | | | | |
| M. | | | | | |
| N. | | | | | |
| O. | | | | | |
| P. | | | | | |
| Q. | | | | | |
| R. | | | | | |
| S. | | | | | |
| T. | | | | | |
| U. | | | | | |
| V. | | | | | |
| W. | | | | | |
| X. | | | | | |
| Y. | | | | | |
| Z. | | | | | |

This Page Not Used.

**PROBLEM 15-2 ___**

| Cost | Direct Materials Cost | Direct Labor Cost | Factory Overhead Cost | Selling Expense | Administrative Expense |
|---|---|---|---|---|---|
| | **Product Costs** | | | **Period Costs** | |
| A. | | | | | |
| B. | | | | | |
| C. | | | | | |
| D. | | | | | |
| E. | | | | | |
| F. | | | | | |
| G. | | | | | |
| H. | | | | | |
| I. | | | | | |
| J. | | | | | |
| K. | | | | | |
| L. | | | | | |
| M. | | | | | |
| N. | | | | | |
| O. | | | | | |
| P. | | | | | |
| Q. | | | | | |
| R. | | | | | |
| S. | | | | | |
| T. | | | | | |
| U. | | | | | |
| V. | | | | | |
| W. | | | | | |
| X. | | | | | |

14

**This Page Not Used.**

**PROBLEM 15-3 ___**

1. _____

_____

_____

_____

2.

| Cost | Direct | Indirect |
|------|--------|----------|
| A. | | |
| B. | | |
| C. | | |
| D. | | |
| E. | | |
| F. | | |
| G. | | |
| H. | | |
| I. | | |
| J. | | |
| K. | | |
| L. | | |
| M. | | |
| N. | | |
| O. | | |
| P. | | |
| Q. | | |
| R. | | |
| S. | | |
| T. | | |
| U. | | |
| V. | | |
| W. | | |

16

**This Page Not Used.**

**PROBLEM 15-4 ___**

1. _____ **Company**

    **A.** _____

    **B.** _____

    **C.** _____

    **D.** _____

    **E.** _____

    **F.** _____

    _____ **Company**

    **A.** _____

    **B.** _____

    **C.** _____

    **D.** _____

    **E.** _____

    **F.** _____

**PROBLEM 15-4 ___, Continued**

2.

|  | Statement of Cost of Goods Manufactured | | | |
|---|---|---|---|---|
|  |  |  |  |  |
|  |  |  |  |  |
|  |  |  |  |  |
|  |  |  |  |  |
|  |  |  |  |  |
|  |  |  |  |  |
|  |  |  |  |  |
|  |  |  |  |  |
|  |  |  |  |  |
|  |  |  |  |  |
|  |  |  |  |  |
|  |  |  |  |  |
|  |  |  |  |  |
|  |  |  |  |  |
|  |  |  |  |  |
|  |  |  |  |  |
|  |  |  |  |  |
|  |  |  |  |  |
|  |  |  |  |  |
|  |  |  |  |  |
|  |  |  |  |  |
|  |  |  |  |  |
|  |  |  |  |  |

**PROBLEM  15-4 ___ , Concluded**

3.

|  | Income Statement | | | |
|---|---|---|---|---|
|  |  |  |  |  |
|  |  |  |  |  |
|  |  |  |  |  |
|  |  |  |  |  |
|  |  |  |  |  |
|  |  |  |  |  |
|  |  |  |  |  |
|  |  |  |  |  |
|  |  |  |  |  |
|  |  |  |  |  |
|  |  |  |  |  |
|  |  |  |  |  |
|  |  |  |  |  |
|  |  |  |  |  |
|  |  |  |  |  |

**This Page Not Used.**

**PROBLEM 15-5 ___**

1.

*Statement of Cost of Goods Manufactured*

**PROBLEM 15-5 ___, Concluded**

2.

*Income Statement*

## EXERCISE 16-1

A. _____

B. _____

C. _____

D. _____

E. _____

## EXERCISE 16-2

**A.** Cost of goods sold:

|  |  |  |
|---|---|---|
|  |  |  |
|  |  |  |
|  |  |  |
|  |  |  |

**B.** Direct materials cost:

|  |  |  |
|---|---|---|
|  |  |  |
|  |  |  |
|  |  |  |
|  |  |  |

**C.** Direct labor cost:

|  |  |  |
|---|---|---|
|  |  |  |
|  |  |  |
|  |  |  |
|  |  |  |

**EXERCISE 16-3**

**A.**

| RECEIVED | | | ISSUED | | | BALANCE | | | |
|---|---|---|---|---|---|---|---|---|---|
| Receiving Report Number | Quantity | Unit Price | Materials Requisition Number | Quantity | Amount | Date | Quantity | Unit Price | Amount |
| | | | | | | May 1 | 285 | $30.00 | $8,550 |
| 40 | 130 | $32.00 | | | | May 4 | _____ | _____ | _____ |
| | | | | | | | _____ | _____ | _____ |
| | | | 91 | 365 | _____ | May 10 | _____ | _____ | _____ |
| 44 | 110 | 38.00 | | | | May 21 | _____ | _____ | _____ |
| | | | | | | | _____ | _____ | _____ |
| | | | 97 | 100 | _____ | May 27 | _____ | _____ | _____ |

**B.** _____

_____

**C.**

JOURNAL                                   PAGE

| | DATE | | DESCRIPTION | POST. REF. | DEBIT | CREDIT | |
|---|---|---|---|---|---|---|---|
| 1 | | | | | | | 1 |
| 2 | | | | | | | 2 |
| 3 | | | | | | | 3 |
| 4 | | | | | | | 4 |

**D.** _____

_____

_____

_____

_____

_____

_____

**EXERCISE 16-4**

**JOURNAL**                                                              PAGE

| | DATE | | DESCRIPTION | POST. REF. | DEBIT | CREDIT | |
|---|---|---|---|---|---|---|---|
| 1 | | | | | | | 1 |
| 2 | | | | | | | 2 |
| 3 | | | | | | | 3 |
| 4 | | | | | | | 4 |

**EXERCISE 16-5**

**A. and B.**

**JOURNAL**                                                              PAGE

| | DATE | | DESCRIPTION | POST. REF. | DEBIT | CREDIT | |
|---|---|---|---|---|---|---|---|
| 1 | | | | | | | 1 |
| 2 | | | | | | | 2 |
| 3 | | | | | | | 3 |
| 4 | | | | | | | 4 |
| 5 | | | | | | | 5 |
| 6 | | | | | | | 6 |
| 7 | | | | | | | 7 |
| 8 | | | | | | | 8 |
| 9 | | | | | | | 9 |
| 10 | | | | | | | 10 |

**C.**

| | Fabric | Polyester Filling | Lumber | Glue |
|---|---|---|---|---|
| | | | | |
| | | | | |
| | | | | |
| | | | | |
| | | | | |

**EXERCISE 16-6**

**JOURNAL**                                                              PAGE

| | DATE | | DESCRIPTION | POST. REF. | DEBIT | CREDIT | |
|---|---|---|---|---|---|---|---|
| 1 | | | | | | | 1 |
| 2 | | | | | | | 2 |
| 3 | | | | | | | 3 |
| 4 | | | | | | | 4 |

**EXERCISE 16-7**

**A.**

| | | JOURNAL | | | | PAGE | |
|---|---|---|---|---|---|---|---|
| | DATE | DESCRIPTION | POST. REF. | DEBIT | CREDIT | | |
| 1 | | | | | | | 1 |
| 2 | | | | | | | 2 |
| 3 | | | | | | | 3 |
| 4 | | | | | | | 4 |

Supporting calculations:

_____

| | | | | | |
|---|---|---|---|---|---|
| | | | | | |
| | | | | | |
| | | | | | |
| | | | | | |

**B.** _____

_____

_____

_____

_____

**EXERCISE 16-8**

**A. and B.**

### JOURNAL

PAGE _____

| | DATE | | DESCRIPTION | POST. REF. | DEBIT | CREDIT | |
|---|---|---|---|---|---|---|---|
| 1 | | | | | | | 1 |
| 2 | | | | | | | 2 |
| 3 | | | | | | | 3 |
| 4 | | | | | | | 4 |
| 5 | | | | | | | 5 |
| 6 | | | | | | | 6 |
| 7 | | | | | | | 7 |
| 8 | | | | | | | 8 |
| 9 | | | | | | | 9 |
| 10 | | | | | | | 10 |

**EXERCISE 16-9**

**A.** Factory 1 overhead rate: _____

_____

**B.** Factory 2 overhead rate: _____

_____

**C.**

### JOURNAL

PAGE _____

| | DATE | | DESCRIPTION | POST. REF. | DEBIT | CREDIT | |
|---|---|---|---|---|---|---|---|
| 1 | | | | | | | 1 |
| 2 | | | | | | | 2 |
| 3 | | | | | | | 3 |
| 4 | | | | | | | 4 |
| 5 | | | | | | | 5 |
| 6 | | | | | | | 6 |
| 7 | | | | | | | 7 |
| 8 | | | | | | | 8 |
| 9 | | | | | | | 9 |

**D.** Balance of Factory 1 accounts as of March 31: _____

_____

Balance of Factory 2 accounts as of March 31: _____

_____

**EXERCISE 16-10**

**EXERCISE 16-11**

A. _____

    _____

    _____

    _____

    _____

    _____

    _____

    _____

B. _____

C.

**EXERCISE 16-12**

**A.**

JOURNAL

| | DATE | | DESCRIPTION | POST. REF. | DEBIT | CREDIT | |
|---|---|---|---|---|---|---|---|
| 1 | | | | | | | 1 |
| 2 | | | | | | | 2 |
| 3 | | | | | | | 3 |
| 4 | | | | | | | 4 |

**B.**

| | | | |
|---|---|---|---|
| | | | |
| | | | |
| | | | |
| | | | |
| | | | |
| | | | |
| | | | |
| | | | |
| | | | |
| | | | |
| | | | |

**EXERCISE 16-13**

**A. through D.**

**JOURNAL**

| | DATE | DESCRIPTION | POST. REF. | DEBIT | CREDIT | |
|---|---|---|---|---|---|---|
| 1 | | | | | | 1 |
| 2 | | | | | | 2 |
| 3 | | | | | | 3 |
| 4 | | | | | | 4 |
| 5 | | | | | | 5 |
| 6 | | | | | | 6 |
| 7 | | | | | | 7 |
| 8 | | | | | | 8 |
| 9 | | | | | | 9 |
| 10 | | | | | | 10 |
| 11 | | | | | | 11 |
| 12 | | | | | | 12 |
| 13 | | | | | | 13 |
| 14 | | | | | | 14 |
| 15 | | | | | | 15 |
| 16 | | | | | | 16 |
| 17 | | | | | | 17 |
| 18 | | | | | | 18 |
| 19 | | | | | | 19 |
| 20 | | | | | | 20 |
| 21 | | | | | | 21 |
| 22 | | | | | | 22 |
| 23 | | | | | | 23 |
| 24 | | | | | | 24 |
| 25 | | | | | | 25 |
| 26 | | | | | | 26 |
| 27 | | | | | | 27 |
| 28 | | | | | | 28 |

**EXERCISE 16-14**

**A.**

|  | Income Statement |  |  |
|---|---|---|---|
|  |  |  |  |
|  |  |  |  |
|  |  |  |  |
|  |  |  |  |
|  |  |  |  |
|  |  |  |  |
|  |  |  |  |
|  |  |  |  |
|  |  |  |  |

**B.** Materials inventory:

|  |  |
|---|---|
|  |  |
|  |  |
|  |  |
|  |  |

Work in process inventory:

|  |  |
|---|---|
|  |  |
|  |  |
|  |  |
|  |  |
|  |  |
|  |  |

Finished goods inventory:

|  |  |
|---|---|
|  |  |
|  |  |
|  |  |
|  |  |

**EXERCISE 16-15**

**A.**

**JOURNAL**

PAGE

| | DATE | | DESCRIPTION | POST. REF. | DEBIT | CREDIT | |
|---|---|---|---|---|---|---|---|
| 1 | | | | | | | 1 |
| 2 | | | | | | | 2 |
| 3 | | | | | | | 3 |
| 4 | | | | | | | 4 |
| 5 | | | | | | | 5 |
| 6 | | | | | | | 6 |
| 7 | | | | | | | 7 |
| 8 | | | | | | | 8 |
| 9 | | | | | | | 9 |
| 10 | | | | | | | 10 |
| 11 | | | | | | | 11 |
| 12 | | | | | | | 12 |
| 13 | | | | | | | 13 |
| 14 | | | | | | | 14 |
| 15 | | | | | | | 15 |
| 16 | | | | | | | 16 |
| 17 | | | | | | | 17 |
| 18 | | | | | | | 18 |
| 19 | | | | | | | 19 |
| 20 | | | | | | | 20 |
| 21 | | | | | | | 21 |
| 22 | | | | | | | 22 |
| 23 | | | | | | | 23 |
| 24 | | | | | | | 24 |
| 25 | | | | | | | 25 |
| 26 | | | | | | | 26 |
| 27 | | | | | | | 27 |
| 28 | | | | | | | 28 |
| 29 | | | | | | | 29 |
| 30 | | | | | | | 30 |
| 31 | | | | | | | 31 |
| 32 | | | | | | | 32 |
| 33 | | | | | | | 33 |
| 34 | | | | | | | 34 |
| 35 | | | | | | | 35 |

**EXERCISE 16-15, Concluded**

**B.**

| | | |
|---|---|---|
| | | |
| | | |
| | | |
| | | |

**C.**

| | | |
|---|---|---|
| | | |
| | | |
| | | |
| | | |

**EXERCISE 16-16**

**A. through D.**

## JOURNAL

PAGE

| | DATE | | DESCRIPTION | POST. REF. | DEBIT | CREDIT | |
|---|---|---|---|---|---|---|---|
| 1 | | | | | | | 1 |
| 2 | | | | | | | 2 |
| 3 | | | | | | | 3 |
| 4 | | | | | | | 4 |
| 5 | | | | | | | 5 |
| 6 | | | | | | | 6 |
| 7 | | | | | | | 7 |
| 8 | | | | | | | 8 |
| 9 | | | | | | | 9 |
| 10 | | | | | | | 10 |
| 11 | | | | | | | 11 |
| 12 | | | | | | | 12 |
| 13 | | | | | | | 13 |
| 14 | | | | | | | 14 |

Supporting calculations:

| | | |
|---|---|---|
| | | |
| | | |
| | | |
| | | |
| | | |
| | | |
| | | |
| | | |
| | | |
| | | |

**This Page Not Used.**

**PROBLEM 16-1 ___**

**A. through I.**

**JOURNAL**                                                PAGE

| | DATE | | DESCRIPTION | POST. REF. | DEBIT | CREDIT | |
|---|---|---|---|---|---|---|---|
| 1 | | | | | | | 1 |
| 2 | | | | | | | 2 |
| 3 | | | | | | | 3 |
| 4 | | | | | | | 4 |
| 5 | | | | | | | 5 |
| 6 | | | | | | | 6 |
| 7 | | | | | | | 7 |
| 8 | | | | | | | 8 |
| 9 | | | | | | | 9 |
| 10 | | | | | | | 10 |
| 11 | | | | | | | 11 |
| 12 | | | | | | | 12 |
| 13 | | | | | | | 13 |
| 14 | | | | | | | 14 |
| 15 | | | | | | | 15 |
| 16 | | | | | | | 16 |
| 17 | | | | | | | 17 |
| 18 | | | | | | | 18 |
| 19 | | | | | | | 19 |
| 20 | | | | | | | 20 |
| 21 | | | | | | | 21 |
| 22 | | | | | | | 22 |
| 23 | | | | | | | 23 |
| 24 | | | | | | | 24 |
| 25 | | | | | | | 25 |
| 26 | | | | | | | 26 |
| 27 | | | | | | | 27 |
| 28 | | | | | | | 28 |
| 29 | | | | | | | 29 |
| 30 | | | | | | | 30 |
| 31 | | | | | | | 31 |
| 32 | | | | | | | 32 |
| 33 | | | | | | | 33 |
| 34 | | | | | | | 34 |
| 35 | | | | | | | 35 |

**PROBLEM 16-1 ___, Concluded**

## JOURNAL

| | DATE | | DESCRIPTION | POST. REF. | DEBIT | CREDIT | |
|---|---|---|---|---|---|---|---|
| 1 | | | | | | | 1 |
| 2 | | | | | | | 2 |
| 3 | | | | | | | 3 |
| 4 | | | | | | | 4 |
| 5 | | | | | | | 5 |
| 6 | | | | | | | 6 |
| 7 | | | | | | | 7 |
| 8 | | | | | | | 8 |
| 9 | | | | | | | 9 |
| 10 | | | | | | | 10 |
| 11 | | | | | | | 11 |
| 12 | | | | | | | 12 |
| 13 | | | | | | | 13 |
| 14 | | | | | | | 14 |
| 15 | | | | | | | 15 |
| 16 | | | | | | | 16 |
| 17 | | | | | | | 17 |
| 18 | | | | | | | 18 |
| 19 | | | | | | | 19 |
| 20 | | | | | | | 20 |
| 21 | | | | | | | 21 |
| 22 | | | | | | | 22 |
| 23 | | | | | | | 23 |
| 24 | | | | | | | 24 |
| 25 | | | | | | | 25 |
| 26 | | | | | | | 26 |
| 27 | | | | | | | 27 |
| 28 | | | | | | | 28 |
| 29 | | | | | | | 29 |
| 30 | | | | | | | 30 |
| 31 | | | | | | | 31 |
| 32 | | | | | | | 32 |
| 33 | | | | | | | 33 |
| 34 | | | | | | | 34 |
| 35 | | | | | | | 35 |
| 36 | | | | | | | 36 |

**PROBLEM 16-2 ___**

**1. A. through G.**

**JOURNAL** PAGE

| | DATE | | DESCRIPTION | POST. REF. | DEBIT | CREDIT | |
|---|---|---|---|---|---|---|---|
| 1 | | | | | | | 1 |
| 2 | | | | | | | 2 |
| 3 | | | | | | | 3 |
| 4 | | | | | | | 4 |
| 5 | | | | | | | 5 |
| 6 | | | | | | | 6 |
| 7 | | | | | | | 7 |
| 8 | | | | | | | 8 |
| 9 | | | | | | | 9 |
| 10 | | | | | | | 10 |
| 11 | | | | | | | 11 |
| 12 | | | | | | | 12 |
| 13 | | | | | | | 13 |
| 14 | | | | | | | 14 |
| 15 | | | | | | | 15 |
| 16 | | | | | | | 16 |
| 17 | | | | | | | 17 |
| 18 | | | | | | | 18 |
| 19 | | | | | | | 19 |
| 20 | | | | | | | 20 |
| 21 | | | | | | | 21 |
| 22 | | | | | | | 22 |
| 23 | | | | | | | 23 |
| 24 | | | | | | | 24 |
| 25 | | | | | | | 25 |
| 26 | | | | | | | 26 |
| 27 | | | | | | | 27 |
| 28 | | | | | | | 28 |
| 29 | | | | | | | 29 |
| 30 | | | | | | | 30 |
| 31 | | | | | | | 31 |
| 32 | | | | | | | 32 |
| 33 | | | | | | | 33 |
| 34 | | | | | | | 34 |
| 35 | | | | | | | 35 |

**PROBLEM 16-2 ___, Continued**

**F.** Computation of cost of jobs finished:

| | | | | |
|---|---|---|---|---|
| | | | | |
| | | | | |
| | | | | |
| | | | | |
| | | | | |

**G.** Computation of cost of jobs sold:

| | |
|---|---|
| | |
| | |
| | |
| | |

**2.**

*Work in Process*

| | |
|---|---|
| | |
| | |
| | |

*Finished Goods*

| | |
|---|---|
| | |
| | |
| | |

**PROBLEM 16-2 ___, Concluded**

**3.**

*Schedule of Unfinished Jobs*

| JOB | DIRECT MATERIALS | DIRECT LABOR | FACTORY OVERHEAD | TOTAL | |
|-----|-----|-----|-----|-----|-----|
| | | | | | |
| | | | | | |
| | | | | | |
| | | | | | |
| | | | | | |

**4.**

*Schedule of Completed Jobs*

| JOB | DIRECT MATERIALS | DIRECT LABOR | FACTORY OVERHEAD | TOTAL | |
|-----|-----|-----|-----|-----|-----|
| | | | | | |
| | | | | | |
| | | | | | |
| | | | | | |

**This Page Not Used.**

**PROBLEM 16-3 ___**

**1. and 2.**

## JOB ORDER COST SHEET

Customer _____

Date _____

Date wanted _____

Date completed _____

Job No. _____

### ESTIMATE

| Direct Materials | | Amount | Direct Labor | | Amount | Summary | Amount |
|---|---|---|---|---|---|---|---|
| ____ meters at $____ | | ____ | ____ hours at $____ | | ____ | Direct materials | ____ |
| ____ meters at | ____ | ____ | ____ hours at | ____ | ____ | Direct labor | ____ |
| ____ meters at | ____ | ____ | ____ hours at | ____ | ____ | Factory overhead | ____ |
| ____ meters at | ____ | ____ | ____ hours at | ____ | | | |
| Total | | ____ | Total | | ____ | Total cost | ____ |

### ACTUAL

| Mat. Req. No. | Description | Amount | Time Ticket No. | Description | Amount | Item | Amount |
|---|---|---|---|---|---|---|---|
| ____ | ____ | ____ | ____ | ____ | ____ | Direct materials | ____ |
| ____ | ____ | ____ | ____ | ____ | ____ | Direct labor | ____ |
| ____ | ____ | ____ | ____ | ____ | ____ | Factory overhead | ____ |
| Total | | ____ | Total | | ____ | Total cost | ____ |

**Comments:**

This Page Not Used.

**PROBLEM 16-4** _____

1. Supporting calculations:

| Job No. | Quantity | Work in Process | Direct Materials | Direct Labor | Factory Overhead | Total Cost | Unit Cost | Units Sold | Cost of Goods Sold |
|---------|----------|-----------------|------------------|--------------|------------------|------------|-----------|------------|--------------------|
|         |          |                 |                  |              |                  |            |           |            |                    |
|         |          |                 |                  |              |                  |            |           |            |                    |
|         |          |                 |                  |              |                  |            |           |            |                    |
|         |          |                 |                  |              |                  |            |           |            |                    |
|         |          |                 |                  |              |                  |            |           |            |                    |
|         |          |                 |                  |              |                  |            |           |            |                    |

A. _____

B. _____

C. _____

D. _____

E. _____

F. _____

G. _____

H. _____

**PROBLEM 16-4 ___, Concluded**

2. _____

_____

_____

_____

_____

_____

_____

_____

_____

_____

_____

_____

_____

_____

_____

_____

_____

_____

_____

**PROBLEM 16-5 ___**

1.

|  | | | |
|---|---|---|---|
| *Income Statement* | | | |
|  | | | |
|  | | | |
|  | | | |
|  | | | |
|  | | | |
|  | | | |
|  | | | |
|  | | | |
|  | | | |
|  | | | |
|  | | | |
|  | | | |
|  | | | |
|  | | | |

Supporting calculations:

_____
_____
_____
_____
_____

|  | | |
|---|---|---|
|  | | |
|  | | |
|  | | |
|  | | |
|  | | |
|  | | |
|  | | |
|  | | |
|  | | |
|  | | |

**PROBLEM 16-5 ___, Concluded**

2. _____

_____

_____

_____

_____

_____

_____

_____

_____

_____

_____

_____

**EXERCISE 17-1**

**A. through E.**

## JOURNAL                                                              PAGE

| | DATE | DESCRIPTION | POST. REF. | DEBIT | CREDIT | |
|---|---|---|---|---|---|---|
| 1 | | | | | | 1 |
| 2 | | | | | | 2 |
| 3 | | | | | | 3 |
| 4 | | | | | | 4 |
| 5 | | | | | | 5 |
| 6 | | | | | | 6 |
| 7 | | | | | | 7 |
| 8 | | | | | | 8 |
| 9 | | | | | | 9 |
| 10 | | | | | | 10 |
| 11 | | | | | | 11 |
| 12 | | | | | | 12 |
| 13 | | | | | | 13 |
| 14 | | | | | | 14 |
| 15 | | | | | | 15 |
| 16 | | | | | | 16 |
| 17 | | | | | | 17 |
| 18 | | | | | | 18 |
| 19 | | | | | | 19 |
| 20 | | | | | | 20 |
| 21 | | | | | | 21 |
| 22 | | | | | | 22 |
| 23 | | | | | | 23 |
| 24 | | | | | | 24 |
| 25 | | | | | | 25 |

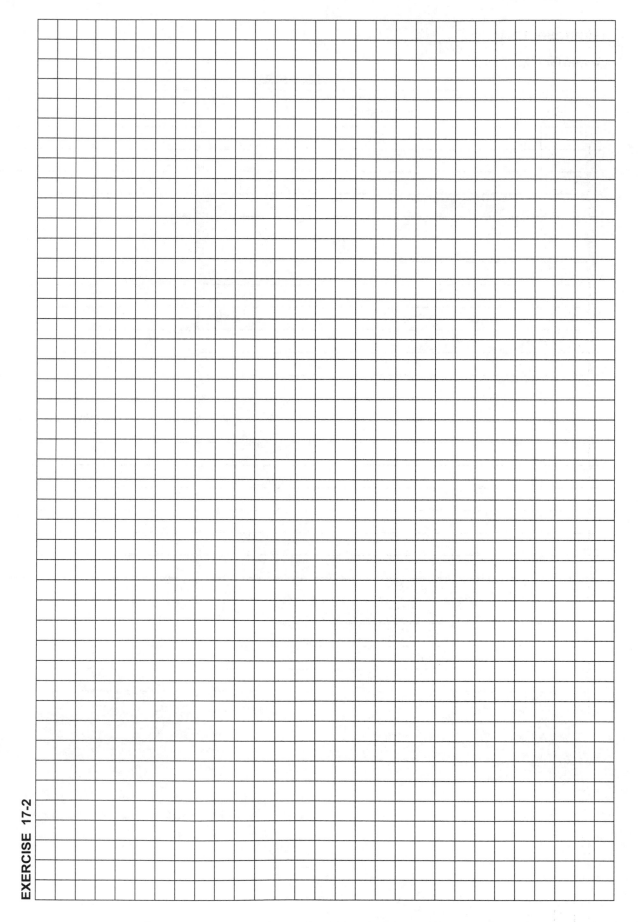

**EXERCISE 17-3**

**A. and B.**

**JOURNAL**                                                    PAGE

| | DATE | | DESCRIPTION | POST. REF. | DEBIT | CREDIT | |
|---|---|---|---|---|---|---|---|
| 1 | | | | | | | 1 |
| 2 | | | | | | | 2 |
| 3 | | | | | | | 3 |
| 4 | | | | | | | 4 |
| 5 | | | | | | | 5 |
| 6 | | | | | | | 6 |
| 7 | | | | | | | 7 |
| 8 | | | | | | | 8 |
| 9 | | | | | | | 9 |
| 10 | | | | | | | 10 |
| 11 | | | | | | | 11 |
| 12 | | | | | | | 12 |
| 13 | | | | | | | 13 |
| 14 | | | | | | | 14 |
| 15 | | | | | | | 15 |
| 16 | | | | | | | 16 |
| 17 | | | | | | | 17 |
| 18 | | | | | | | 18 |
| 19 | | | | | | | 19 |
| 20 | | | | | | | 20 |

## EXERCISE 17-4

A. _____

_____

B.

**JOURNAL**                                                      PAGE

| | DATE | DESCRIPTION | POST. REF. | DEBIT | CREDIT | |
|---|---|---|---|---|---|---|
| 1 | | | | | | 1 |
| 2 | | | | | | 2 |
| 3 | | | | | | 3 |
| 4 | | | | | | 4 |
| 5 | | | | | | 5 |
| 6 | | | | | | 6 |
| 7 | | | | | | 7 |

C. _____

D. _____

## EXERCISE 17-5

| | A | B | C | D |
|---|---|---|---|---|
| 1 | | | Equivalent Units | |
| 2 | | Whole Units | Direct Materials | Conversion |
| 3 | | | | |
| 4 | | | | |
| 5 | | | | |
| 6 | | | | |
| 7 | | | | |
| 8 | | | | |
| 9 | | | | |
| 10 | | | | |
| 11 | | | | |
| 12 | | | | |
| 13 | | | | |
| 14 | | | | |
| 15 | | | | |
| 16 | | | | |

**EXERCISE 17-6**

**A.** Drawing Department

| | A | B | C | D |
|---|---|---|---|---|
| | | | Equivalent Units | |
| 1 | | | Direct Materials | Conversion |
| 2 | | Whole Units | | |
| 3 | | | | |
| 4 | | | | |
| 5 | | | | |
| 6 | | | | |
| 7 | | | | |
| 8 | | | | |
| 9 | | | | |
| 10 | | | | |
| 11 | | | | |
| 12 | | | | |
| 13 | | | | |
| 14 | | | | |
| 15 | | | | |
| 16 | | | | |

**B.** Winding Department

| | A | B | C | D |
|---|---|---|---|---|
| | | | Equivalent Units | |
| 1 | | | Direct Materials | Conversion |
| 2 | | Whole Units | | |
| 3 | | | | |
| 4 | | | | |
| 5 | | | | |
| 6 | | | | |
| 7 | | | | |
| 8 | | | | |
| 9 | | | | |
| 10 | | | | |
| 11 | | | | |
| 12 | | | | |
| 13 | | | | |
| 14 | | | | |
| 15 | | | | |
| 16 | | | | |

**EXERCISE 17-7**

**A.**

| | |
|---|---|
| | |
| | |
| | |
| | |

**EXERCISE 17-7, Concluded**

**B.**

| A | B | Equivalent Units | |
|---|---|---|---|
|   | Whole Units | Direct Materials | Conversion |
| 3 |   |   |   |
| 4 |   |   |   |
| 5 |   |   |   |
| 6 |   |   |   |
| 7 |   |   |   |
| 8 |   |   |   |
| 9 |   |   |   |
| 10 |   |   |   |
| 11 |   |   |   |
| 12 |   |   |   |
| 13 |   |   |   |
| 14 |   |   |   |
| 15 |   |   |   |
| 16 |   |   |   |

**EXERCISE 17-8**

A. 1. _____

   2. _____

   3. _____

   4. _____

   5. _____

**EXERCISE 17-8,  Concluded**

**B.** _____

_____

| | | |
|---|---|---|
| | | |
| | | |
| | | |
| | | |
| | | |
| | | |
| | | |
| | | |
| | | |
| | | |
| | | |
| | | |
| | | |
| | | |
| | | |
| | | |
| | | |
| | | |
| | | |

## EXERCISE 17-9

Equivalent units of production:

|  | CEREAL (IN POUNDS) | BOXES (IN BOXES) | CONVERSION COST (IN BOXES) |
|---|---|---|---|
|  |  |  |  |
|  |  |  |  |
|  |  |  |  |
|  |  |  |  |
|  |  |  |  |
|  |  |  |  |
|  |  |  |  |
|  |  |  |  |

Supporting explanation:

_____

_____

_____

_____

_____

_____

_____

_____

_____

_____

_____

_____

_____

_____

_____

_____

_____

_____

_____

_____

_____

_____

_____

**EXERCISE 17-10**

**A.**

**B.**

**C.**

**EXERCISE 17-11**

**A.**

| | | |
|---|---|---|
| | | |
| | | |
| | | |
| | | |
| | | |
| | | |

**B.**

| | A | B | C | D |
|---|---|---|---|---|
| 1 | | | Equivalent Units | |
| 2 | | Whole Units | Direct Materials | Conversion |
| 3 | | | | |
| 4 | | | | |
| 5 | | | | |
| 6 | | | | |
| 7 | | | | |
| 8 | | | | |
| 9 | | | | |
| 10 | | | | |
| 11 | | | | |
| 12 | | | | |
| 13 | | | | |
| 14 | | | | |

**C.**

| | A | B | C |
|---|---|---|---|
| 1 | | Costs | |
| 2 | | Direct Materials | Conversion |
| 3 | | | |
| 4 | | | |
| 5 | | | |
| 6 | | | |
| 7 | | | |
| 8 | | | |
| 9 | | | |
| 10 | | | |

**D.** _____

**EXERCISE 17-12**

A. 1. _____

| | | |
|---|---|---|
| | | |
| | | |
| | | |
| | | |
| | | |
| | | |

2. _____

| | | |
|---|---|---|
| | | |
| | | |
| | | |
| | | |
| | | |
| | | |

3. _____

| | | |
|---|---|---|
| | | |
| | | |
| | | |
| | | |
| | | |
| | | |

4. _____

B. _____
_____
_____
_____
_____
_____
_____
_____

**EXERCISE 17-12, Concluded**

C. _____

_____

| | | |
|---|---|---|
| | | |
| | | |
| | | |
| | | |
| | | |
| | | |
| | | |
| | | |
| | | |
| | | |
| | | |
| | | |
| | | |
| | | |
| | | |
| | | |
| | | |
| | | |
| | | |

**EXERCISE 17-13**

**EXERCISE 17-14**

A. _____

B.

| | A | B | Equivalent Units | |
|---|---|---|---|---|
| | | Whole Units | Direct Materials | Conversion |
| 3 | | | | |
| 4 | | | | |
| 5 | | | | |
| 6 | | | | |
| 7 | | | | |
| 8 | | | | |
| 9 | | | | |
| 10 | | | | |
| 11 | | | | |
| 12 | | | | |
| 13 | | | | |
| 14 | | | | |
| 15 | | | | |
| 16 | | | | |

| | A | Costs | |
|---|---|---|---|
| | | Direct Materials | Conversion |
| 3 | | | |
| 4 | | | |
| 5 | | | |
| 6 | | | |
| 7 | | | |
| 8 | | | |
| 9 | | | |
| 10 | | | |

C. _____

**EXERCISE 17-15**

A. _____

B. _____

C. _____

D. _____

E. _____

**EXERCISE 17-16**

**A.  1. through 4.**

| | A | B | C | D |
|---|---|---|---|---|
| 1 | | | | |
| 2 | Cost of Production Report—_____ | | | |
| 3 | | | | |
| 4 | | | Equivalent Units | |
| 5 | UNITS | Whole Units | Direct Materials | Conversion |
| 6 | | | | |
| 7 | | | | |
| 8 | | | | |
| 9 | | | | |
| 10 | | | | |
| 11 | | | | |
| 12 | | | | |
| 13 | | | | |
| 14 | | | | |
| 15 | | | | |
| 16 | | | | |
| 17 | | | | |
| 18 | | | | |
| 19 | | | | |
| 20 | | | | |
| 21 | | | | |
| 22 | | | | |
| 23 | | | | |
| 24 | | | | |
| 25 | | | | |
| 26 | | | | |
| 27 | | | | |
| 28 | | | | |
| 29 | | | | |
| 30 | | | | |

**EXERCISE 17-16, Continued**

| | A | B | C | D |
|---|---|---|---|---|
| | | | Costs | |
| | COSTS | Direct Materials | Conversion | Total |
| 3 | | | | |
| 4 | | | | |
| 5 | | | | |
| 6 | | | | |
| 7 | | | | |
| 8 | | | | |
| 9 | | | | |
| 10 | | | | |
| 11 | | | | |
| 12 | | | | |
| 13 | | | | |
| 14 | | | | |
| 15 | | | | |
| 16 | | | | |
| 17 | | | | |
| 18 | | | | |
| 19 | | | | |
| 20 | | | | |
| 21 | | | | |
| 22 | | | | |
| 23 | | | | |
| 24 | | | | |
| 25 | | | | |
| 26 | | | | |
| 27 | | | | |
| 28 | | | | |
| 29 | | | | |
| 30 | | | | |
| 31 | | | | |
| 32 | | | | |
| 33 | | | | |
| 34 | | | | |
| 35 | | | | |
| 36 | | | | |
| 37 | | | | |
| 38 | | | | |
| 39 | | | | |
| 40 | | | | |
| 41 | | | | |
| 42 | | | | |

**EXERCISE 17-16, Concluded**

**B.**

**EXERCISE 17-17**

**A.**

| | A | B | C | D |
|---|---|---|---|---|
| 1 | | | | |
| 2 | Cost of Production Report—_____ | | | |
| 3 | | | | |
| 4 | | | Equivalent Units | |
| 5 | UNITS | Whole Units | Direct Materials | Conversion |
| 6 | | | | |
| 7 | | | | |
| 8 | | | | |
| 9 | | | | |
| 10 | | | | |
| 11 | | | | |
| 12 | | | | |
| 13 | | | | |
| 14 | | | | |
| 15 | | | | |
| 16 | | | | |
| 17 | | | | |
| 18 | | | | |
| 19 | | | | |
| 20 | | | | |
| 21 | | | | |
| 22 | | | | |
| 23 | | | | |
| 24 | | | | |
| 25 | | | | |
| 26 | | | | |
| 27 | | | | |
| 28 | | | | |
| 29 | | | | |
| 30 | | | | |

**EXERCISE 17-17, Continued**

| | A | B | C | D |
|---|---|---|---|---|
| 1 | | | Costs | |
| 2 | COSTS | Direct Materials | Conversion | Total |
| 3 | | | | |
| 4 | | | | |
| 5 | | | | |
| 6 | | | | |
| 7 | | | | |
| 8 | | | | |
| 9 | | | | |
| 10 | | | | |
| 11 | | | | |
| 12 | | | | |
| 13 | | | | |
| 14 | | | | |
| 15 | | | | |
| 16 | | | | |
| 17 | | | | |
| 18 | | | | |
| 19 | | | | |
| 20 | | | | |
| 21 | | | | |
| 22 | | | | |
| 23 | | | | |
| 24 | | | | |
| 25 | | | | |
| 26 | | | | |
| 27 | | | | |
| 28 | | | | |
| 29 | | | | |
| 30 | | | | |
| 31 | | | | |
| 32 | | | | |
| 33 | | | | |
| 34 | | | | |
| 35 | | | | |
| 36 | | | | |
| 37 | | | | |
| 38 | | | | |
| 39 | | | | |
| 40 | | | | |
| 41 | | | | |
| 42 | | | | |

**EXERCISE 17-17, Concluded**

**B.**

| | | |
|---|---|---|
| | | |
| | | |
| | | |
| | | |
| | | |
| | | |
| | | |

**EXERCISE 17-18**

**A. 1. through 3.**

**JOURNAL**                                              PAGE

| | DATE | DESCRIPTION | POST. REF. | DEBIT | CREDIT | |
|---|---|---|---|---|---|---|
| 1 | | | | | | 1 |
| 2 | | | | | | 2 |
| 3 | | | | | | 3 |
| 4 | | | | | | 4 |
| 5 | | | | | | 5 |
| 6 | | | | | | 6 |
| 7 | | | | | | 7 |
| 8 | | | | | | 8 |
| 9 | | | | | | 9 |
| 10 | | | | | | 10 |
| 11 | | | | | | 11 |
| 12 | | | | | | 12 |
| 13 | | | | | | 13 |
| 14 | | | | | | 14 |
| 15 | | | | | | 15 |
| 16 | | | | | | 16 |
| 17 | | | | | | 17 |
| 18 | | | | | | 18 |

**EXERCISE 17-18, Continued**

Supporting calculations:

| | | | | |
|---|---|---|---|---|
| | | | | |
| | | | | |
| | | | | |
| | | | | |
| | | | | |
| | | | | |
| | | | | |
| | | | | |
| | | | | |

| | A | B | Equivalent Units | |
|---|---|---|---|---|
| | | **Whole Units** | **Direct Materials** | **Conversion** |
| 1 | | | | |
| 2 | | | | |
| 3 | | | | |
| 4 | | | | |
| 5 | | | | |
| 6 | | | | |
| 7 | | | | |
| 8 | | | | |
| 9 | | | | |
| 10 | | | | |
| 11 | | | | |
| 12 | | | | |
| 13 | | | | |
| 14 | | | | |
| 15 | | | | |
| 16 | | | | |
| 17 | | | | |
| 18 | | | | |

_____

_____

_____

_____

_____

_____

**EXERCISE 17-18, Concluded**

**B.** _____

| | | |
|---|---|---|
| | | |
| | | |
| | | |
| | | |

_____

_____

**C.**

| | | |
|---|---|---|
| | | |
| | | |
| | | |
| | | |
| | | |
| | | |
| | | |

_____

_____

_____

_____

_____

_____

**EXERCISE 17-19**

**A. 1. through 3.**

JOURNAL

PAGE

| | DATE | | DESCRIPTION | POST. REF. | DEBIT | CREDIT | |
|---|---|---|---|---|---|---|---|
| 1 | | | | | | | 1 |
| 2 | | | | | | | 2 |
| 3 | | | | | | | 3 |
| 4 | | | | | | | 4 |
| 5 | | | | | | | 5 |
| 6 | | | | | | | 6 |
| 7 | | | | | | | 7 |
| 8 | | | | | | | 8 |
| 9 | | | | | | | 9 |
| 10 | | | | | | | 10 |
| 11 | | | | | | | 11 |
| 12 | | | | | | | 12 |
| 13 | | | | | | | 13 |
| 14 | | | | | | | 14 |
| 15 | | | | | | | 15 |

**EXERCISE 17-19, Continued**

Supporting calculations:

| | |
|---|---|
| | |
| | |
| | |
| | |
| | |
| | |
| | |
| | |
| | |
| | |

| | A | B | C | D |
|---|---|---|---|---|
| 1 | | | Equivalent Units | |
| 2 | | Whole Units | Direct Materials | Conversion |
| 3 | | | | |
| 4 | | | | |
| 5 | | | | |
| 6 | | | | |
| 7 | | | | |
| 8 | | | | |
| 9 | | | | |
| 10 | | | | |
| 11 | | | | |
| 12 | | | | |
| 13 | | | | |
| 14 | | | | |
| 15 | | | | |

**EXERCISE 17-19, Concluded**

B. _____

**EXERCISE 17-20**

**A.** Cost per megawatt hour (MWh) for the fossil fuel plant:

| | |
|---|---|
| | |
| | |
| | |
| | |
| | |
| | |
| | |
| | |

_____
_____
_____

Cost per megawatt hour (MWh) for the wind farm:

| | |
|---|---|
| | |
| | |
| | |
| | |
| | |
| | |
| | |
| | |
| | |

_____
_____
_____

Lowest cost facility:

_____
_____
_____

**EXERCISE 17-20, Concluded**

**B.** _____

_____

_____

_____

_____

_____

_____

_____

_____

_____

**C.** _____

_____

_____

_____

_____

_____

_____

_____

_____

_____

_____

**EXERCISE 17-21**

**EXERCISE 17-21, Concluded**

**APPENDIX EXERCISE 17-22**

**A. and B.**

| | A | B | C |
|---|---|---|---|
| 1 | | **A. Whole Units** | **B. Equivalent Units of Production** |
| 2 | | | |
| 3 | | | |
| 4 | | | |
| 5 | | | |
| 6 | | | |
| 7 | | | |
| 8 | | | |
| 9 | | | |
| 10 | | | |
| 11 | | | |
| 12 | | | |
| 13 | | | |
| 14 | | | |
| 15 | | | |

**APPENDIX EXERCISE 17-23**

**A.** Drawing Department

| | A | B | C |
|---|---|---|---|
| 1 | | **Whole Units** | **Equivalent Units of Production** |
| 2 | | | |
| 3 | | | |
| 4 | | | |
| 5 | | | |
| 6 | | | |
| 7 | | | |
| 8 | | | |
| 9 | | | |
| 10 | | | |
| 11 | | | |
| 12 | | | |
| 13 | | | |
| 14 | | | |
| 15 | | | |

## APPENDIX EXERCISE 17-23, Concluded

**B.** Winding Department

| | A | B | C |
|---|---|---|---|
| 1 | | **Whole Units** | **Equivalent Units of Production** |
| 2 | | | |
| 3 | | | |
| 4 | | | |
| 5 | | | |
| 6 | | | |
| 7 | | | |
| 8 | | | |
| 9 | | | |
| 10 | | | |
| 11 | | | |
| 12 | | | |
| 13 | | | |
| 14 | | | |
| 15 | | | |

## APPENDIX EXERCISE 17-24

**A.**

| | | |
|---|---|---|
| | | |
| | | |
| | | |
| | | |

**B.**

| | A | B | C |
|---|---|---|---|
| 1 | | **Whole Units** | **Equivalent Units of Production** |
| 2 | | | |
| 3 | | | |
| 4 | | | |
| 5 | | | |
| 6 | | | |
| 7 | | | |
| 8 | | | |
| 9 | | | |
| 10 | | | |
| 11 | | | |
| 12 | | | |
| 13 | | | |
| 14 | | | |
| 15 | | | |

**APPENDIX EXERCISE 17-25**

**A. and B.**

| | A | Whole Units | Equivalent Units of Production |
|---|---|---|---|
| 1 | | | |
| 2 | | | |
| 3 | | | |
| 4 | | | |
| 5 | | | |
| 6 | | | |
| 7 | | | |
| 8 | | | |
| 9 | | | |
| 10 | | | |
| 11 | | | |
| 12 | | | |
| 13 | | | |
| 14 | | | |
| 15 | | | |

**C.** _____

_____

_____

_____

_____

_____

_____

_____

**D.** _____

_____

**E.** _____

_____

**APPENDIX EXERCISE 17-26**

**A.**

|  | Whole Units | Equivalent Units of Production |
|---|---|---|
| | | |
| | | |
| | | |
| | | |
| | | |
| | | |
| | | |
| | | |
| | | |
| | | |
| | | |
| | | |
| | | |
| | | |

_____

_____

_____

_____

_____

_____

_____

_____

**B.** _____

_____

**C.** _____

_____

**APPENDIX EXERCISE 17-27**

|   | A | B | C |
|---|---|---|---|
| 1 | | | |
| 2 | Cost of Production Report—_____ | | |
| 3 | | | |
| 4 | UNITS | Whole Units | Equivalent Units of Production |
| 5 | | | |
| 6 | | | |
| 7 | | | |
| 8 | | | |
| 9 | | | |
| 10 | | | |
| 11 | | | |
| 12 | | | |
| 13 | | | |
| 14 | | | |
| 15 | | | |
| 16 | | | |
| 17 | | | |
| 18 | | | |
| 19 | | | |
| 20 | | | |

|   | A | B |
|---|---|---|
| 1 | COSTS | Costs |
| 2 | | |
| 3 | | |
| 4 | | |
| 5 | | |
| 6 | | |
| 7 | | |
| 8 | | |
| 9 | | |
| 10 | | |
| 11 | | |
| 12 | | |
| 13 | | |
| 14 | | |
| 15 | | |
| 16 | | |
| 17 | | |
| 18 | | |
| 19 | | |
| 20 | | |
| 21 | | |
| 22 | | |

**APPENDIX EXERCISE 17-28**

| | A | B | C |
|---|---|---|---|
| 1 | | | |
| 2 | Cost of Production Report—_____ | | |
| 3 | | | |
| 4 | UNITS | Whole Units | Equivalent Units of Production |
| 5 | | | |
| 6 | | | |
| 7 | | | |
| 8 | | | |
| 9 | | | |
| 10 | | | |
| 11 | | | |
| 12 | | | |
| 13 | | | |
| 14 | | | |
| 15 | | | |
| 16 | | | |
| 17 | | | |
| 18 | | | |

| | A | B |
|---|---|---|
| 1 | COSTS | Costs |
| 2 | | |
| 3 | | |
| 4 | | |
| 5 | | |
| 6 | | |
| 7 | | |
| 8 | | |
| 9 | | |
| 10 | | |
| 11 | | |
| 12 | | |
| 13 | | |
| 14 | | |
| 15 | | |
| 16 | | |
| 17 | | |
| 18 | | |
| 19 | | |
| 20 | | |
| 21 | | |
| 22 | | |
| 23 | | |
| 24 | | |

**PROBLEM 17-1 ___**

**1. A. through I.**

## JOURNAL                                                    PAGE _____

| | DATE | | DESCRIPTION | POST. REF. | DEBIT | CREDIT | |
|---|---|---|---|---|---|---|---|
| 1 | | | | | | | 1 |
| 2 | | | | | | | 2 |
| 3 | | | | | | | 3 |
| 4 | | | | | | | 4 |
| 5 | | | | | | | 5 |
| 6 | | | | | | | 6 |
| 7 | | | | | | | 7 |
| 8 | | | | | | | 8 |
| 9 | | | | | | | 9 |
| 10 | | | | | | | 10 |
| 11 | | | | | | | 11 |
| 12 | | | | | | | 12 |
| 13 | | | | | | | 13 |
| 14 | | | | | | | 14 |
| 15 | | | | | | | 15 |
| 16 | | | | | | | 16 |
| 17 | | | | | | | 17 |
| 18 | | | | | | | 18 |
| 19 | | | | | | | 19 |
| 20 | | | | | | | 20 |
| 21 | | | | | | | 21 |
| 22 | | | | | | | 22 |
| 23 | | | | | | | 23 |
| 24 | | | | | | | 24 |
| 25 | | | | | | | 25 |
| 26 | | | | | | | 26 |
| 27 | | | | | | | 27 |
| 28 | | | | | | | 28 |
| 29 | | | | | | | 29 |
| 30 | | | | | | | 30 |
| 31 | | | | | | | 31 |
| 32 | | | | | | | 32 |
| 33 | | | | | | | 33 |
| 34 | | | | | | | 34 |
| 35 | | | | | | | 35 |

**PROBLEM 17-1 ___ , Continued**

**JOURNAL**                                    PAGE _____

| | DATE | DESCRIPTION | POST. REF. | DEBIT | CREDIT | |
|---|---|---|---|---|---|---|
| 1 | | | | | | 1 |
| 2 | | | | | | 2 |
| 3 | | | | | | 3 |
| 4 | | | | | | 4 |
| 5 | | | | | | 5 |
| 6 | | | | | | 6 |
| 7 | | | | | | 7 |
| 8 | | | | | | 8 |
| 9 | | | | | | 9 |
| 10 | | | | | | 10 |
| 11 | | | | | | 11 |
| 12 | | | | | | 12 |
| 13 | | | | | | 13 |
| 14 | | | | | | 14 |
| 15 | | | | | | 15 |
| 16 | | | | | | 16 |
| 17 | | | | | | 17 |
| 18 | | | | | | 18 |
| 19 | | | | | | 19 |
| 20 | | | | | | 20 |
| 21 | | | | | | 21 |
| 22 | | | | | | 22 |
| 23 | | | | | | 23 |
| 24 | | | | | | 24 |
| 25 | | | | | | 25 |
| 26 | | | | | | 26 |
| 27 | | | | | | 27 |
| 28 | | | | | | 28 |
| 29 | | | | | | 29 |
| 30 | | | | | | 30 |
| 31 | | | | | | 31 |
| 32 | | | | | | 32 |
| 33 | | | | | | 33 |
| 34 | | | | | | 34 |
| 35 | | | | | | 35 |
| 36 | | | | | | 36 |

**PROBLEM 17-1 ___, Concluded**

2.

| | MATERIALS | WORK IN PROCESS—_____ DEPT. | WORK IN PROCESS—_____ DEPT. | FINISHED GOODS | |
|---|---|---|---|---|---|
| | | | | | |
| | | | | | |
| | | | | | |
| | | | | | |
| | | | | | |
| | | | | | |
| | | | | | |

3.

| | FACTORY OVERHEAD—_____ DEPT. | FACTORY OVERHEAD—_____ DEPT. | |
|---|---|---|---|
| | | | |
| | | | |
| | | | |
| | | | |
| | | | |
| | | | |
| | | | |

**This Page Not Used.**

**PROBLEM 17-2 ___**

1.

| | A | B | C | D |
|---|---|---|---|---|
| 1 | | | | |
| 2 | **Cost of Production Report—**_____ | | | |
| 3 | | | | |
| 4 | | | **Equivalent Units** | |
| 5 | **UNITS** | **Whole Units** | **Direct Materials** | **Conversion** |
| 6 | | | | |
| 7 | | | | |
| 8 | | | | |
| 9 | | | | |
| 10 | | | | |
| 11 | | | | |
| 12 | | | | |
| 13 | | | | |
| 14 | | | | |
| 15 | | | | |
| 16 | | | | |
| 17 | | | | |
| 18 | | | | |
| 19 | | | | |
| 20 | | | | |
| 21 | | | | |
| 22 | | | | |
| 23 | | | | |
| 24 | | | | |
| 25 | | | | |
| 26 | | | | |
| 27 | | | | |
| 28 | | | | |
| 29 | | | | |
| 30 | | | | |
| 31 | | | | |
| 32 | | | | |
| 33 | | | | |
| 34 | | | | |
| 35 | | | | |
| 36 | | | | |
| 37 | | | | |
| 38 | | | | |
| 39 | | | | |
| 40 | | | | |
| 41 | | | | |
| 42 | | | | |

**PROBLEM 17-2 ___, Continued**

| | A | B | C | D |
|---|---|---|---|---|
| | | | Costs | |
| | COSTS | Direct Materials | Conversion | Total |
| 3 | | | | |
| 4 | | | | |
| 5 | | | | |
| 6 | | | | |
| 7 | | | | |
| 8 | | | | |
| 9 | | | | |
| 10 | | | | |
| 11 | | | | |
| 12 | | | | |
| 13 | | | | |
| 14 | | | | |
| 15 | | | | |
| 16 | | | | |
| 17 | | | | |
| 18 | | | | |
| 19 | | | | |
| 20 | | | | |
| 21 | | | | |
| 22 | | | | |
| 23 | | | | |
| 24 | | | | |
| 25 | | | | |
| 26 | | | | |
| 27 | | | | |
| 28 | | | | |
| 29 | | | | |
| 30 | | | | |
| 31 | | | | |
| 32 | | | | |
| 33 | | | | |
| 34 | | | | |
| 35 | | | | |
| 36 | | | | |
| 37 | | | | |
| 38 | | | | |
| 39 | | | | |
| 40 | | | | |
| 41 | | | | |
| 42 | | | | |

**PROBLEM  17-2 ___ ,  Concluded**

2. _____

_____

_____

_____

_____

_____

_____

_____

_____

_____

_____

Computations:

|  |  |  |
|---|---|---|
|  |  |  |
|  |  |  |
|  |  |  |
|  |  |  |
|  |  |  |
|  |  |  |

**This Page Not Used.**

**PROBLEM 17-3 ___**

1.

| | A | B | C | D |
|---|---|---|---|---|
| 1 | | | | |
| 2 | Cost of Production Report—_____ | | | |
| 3 | | | | |
| 4 | | | Equivalent Units | |
| 5 | UNITS | Whole Units | Direct Materials | Conversion |
| 6 | | | | |
| 7 | | | | |
| 8 | | | | |
| 9 | | | | |
| 10 | | | | |
| 11 | | | | |
| 12 | | | | |
| 13 | | | | |
| 14 | | | | |
| 15 | | | | |
| 16 | | | | |
| 17 | | | | |
| 18 | | | | |
| 19 | | | | |
| 20 | | | | |
| 21 | | | | |
| 22 | | | | |
| 23 | | | | |
| 24 | | | | |
| 25 | | | | |
| 26 | | | | |
| 27 | | | | |
| 28 | | | | |
| 29 | | | | |
| 30 | | | | |
| 31 | | | | |
| 32 | | | | |
| 33 | | | | |
| 34 | | | | |
| 35 | | | | |
| 36 | | | | |
| 37 | | | | |
| 38 | | | | |
| 39 | | | | |
| 40 | | | | |
| 41 | | | | |
| 42 | | | | |

**PROBLEM 17-3 \_\_\_ , Continued**

| | A | B | C | D |
|---|---|---|---|---|
| 1 | | Costs | | |
| 2 | COSTS | Direct Materials | Conversion | Total |
| 3 | | | | |
| 4 | | | | |
| 5 | | | | |
| 6 | | | | |
| 7 | | | | |
| 8 | | | | |
| 9 | | | | |
| 10 | | | | |
| 11 | | | | |
| 12 | | | | |
| 13 | | | | |
| 14 | | | | |
| 15 | | | | |
| 16 | | | | |
| 17 | | | | |
| 18 | | | | |
| 19 | | | | |
| 20 | | | | |
| 21 | | | | |
| 22 | | | | |
| 23 | | | | |
| 24 | | | | |
| 25 | | | | |
| 26 | | | | |
| 27 | | | | |
| 28 | | | | |
| 29 | | | | |
| 30 | | | | |
| 31 | | | | |
| 32 | | | | |
| 33 | | | | |
| 34 | | | | |
| 35 | | | | |
| 36 | | | | |
| 37 | | | | |
| 38 | | | | |
| 39 | | | | |
| 40 | | | | |
| 41 | | | | |
| 42 | | | | |

**PROBLEM 17-3 ___, Concluded**

2.

JOURNAL PAGE

| | DATE | | DESCRIPTION | POST. REF. | DEBIT | CREDIT | |
|---|---|---|---|---|---|---|---|
| 1 | | | | | | | 1 |
| 2 | | | | | | | 2 |
| 3 | | | | | | | 3 |
| 4 | | | | | | | 4 |
| 5 | | | | | | | 5 |
| 6 | | | | | | | 6 |
| 7 | | | | | | | 7 |
| 8 | | | | | | | 8 |
| 9 | | | | | | | 9 |
| 10 | | | | | | | 10 |

3. _____

_____

4. _____

_____

_____

_____

_____

_____

_____

_____

_____

_____

_____

**This Page Not Used.**

**PROBLEM 17-4 ___**

**1. and 2.**

ACCOUNT     *Work in Process—_____*        ACCOUNT NO.

| DATE | ITEM | DEBIT | CREDIT | BALANCE DEBIT | CREDIT |
|---|---|---|---|---|---|
|  |  |  |  |  |  |
|  |  |  |  |  |  |
|  |  |  |  |  |  |
|  |  |  |  |  |  |
|  |  |  |  |  |  |
|  |  |  |  |  |  |
|  |  |  |  |  |  |
|  |  |  |  |  |  |
|  |  |  |  |  |  |
|  |  |  |  |  |  |
|  |  |  |  |  |  |
|  |  |  |  |  |  |
|  |  |  |  |  |  |
|  |  |  |  |  |  |
|  |  |  |  |  |  |
|  |  |  |  |  |  |
|  |  |  |  |  |  |
|  |  |  |  |  |  |
|  |  |  |  |  |  |
|  |  |  |  |  |  |
|  |  |  |  |  |  |
|  |  |  |  |  |  |
|  |  |  |  |  |  |
|  |  |  |  |  |  |
|  |  |  |  |  |  |
|  |  |  |  |  |  |
|  |  |  |  |  |  |
|  |  |  |  |  |  |
|  |  |  |  |  |  |

**PROBLEM 17-4 ___, Continued**

1.

| | A | B | C | D |
|---|---|---|---|---|
| 1 | | | | |
| 2 | Cost of Production Report—_____ | | | |
| 3 | | | | |
| 4 | | | Equivalent Units | |
| 5 | UNITS | Whole Units | Direct Materials (A) | Conversion (A) |
| 6 | | | | |
| 7 | | | | |
| 8 | | | | |
| 9 | | | | |
| 10 | | | | |
| 11 | | | | |
| 12 | | | | |
| 13 | | | | |
| 14 | | | | |
| 15 | | | | |
| 16 | | | | |
| 17 | | | | |
| 18 | | | | |
| 19 | | | | |
| 20 | | | | |
| 21 | | | | |
| 22 | | | | |
| 23 | | | | |
| 24 | | | | |
| 25 | | | | |
| 26 | | | | |
| 27 | | | | |
| 28 | | | | |
| 29 | | | | |
| 30 | | | | |
| 31 | | | | |
| 32 | | | | |
| 33 | | | | |
| 34 | | | | |
| 35 | | | | |
| 36 | | | | |
| 37 | | | | |
| 38 | | | | |
| 39 | | | | |
| 40 | | | | |
| 41 | | | | |
| 42 | | | | |

**PROBLEM 17-4 ___, Continued**

| | COSTS | Costs | | |
|---|---|---|---|---|
| | | Direct Materials | Conversion | Total |
| 3 | | | | |
| 4 | | | | |
| 5 | | | | |
| 6 | | | | |
| 7 | | | | |
| 8 | | | | |
| 9 | | | | |
| 10 | | | | |
| 11 | | | | |
| 12 | | | | |
| 13 | | | | |
| 14 | | | | |
| 15 | | | | |
| 16 | | | | |
| 17 | | | | |
| 18 | | | | |
| 19 | | | | |
| 20 | | | | |
| 21 | | | | |
| 22 | | | | |
| 23 | | | | |
| 24 | | | | |
| 25 | | | | |
| 26 | | | | |
| 27 | | | | |
| 28 | | | | |
| 29 | | | | |
| 30 | | | | |
| 31 | | | | |
| 32 | | | | |
| 33 | | | | |
| 34 | | | | |
| 35 | | | | |
| 36 | | | | |
| 37 | | | | |
| 38 | | | | |
| 39 | | | | |
| 40 | | | | |
| 41 | | | | |
| 42 | | | | |

**PROBLEM 17-4 ___, Continued**

2.

| | A | B | C | D |
|---|---|---|---|---|
| 1 | | | | |
| 2 | **Cost of Production Report—_____** | | | |
| 3 | | | | |
| 4 | | | **Equivalent Units** | |
| 5 | **UNITS** | **Whole Units** | **Direct Materials (A)** | **Conversion (A)** |
| 6 | | | | |
| 7 | | | | |
| 8 | | | | |
| 9 | | | | |
| 10 | | | | |
| 11 | | | | |
| 12 | | | | |
| 13 | | | | |
| 14 | | | | |
| 15 | | | | |
| 16 | | | | |
| 17 | | | | |
| 18 | | | | |
| 19 | | | | |
| 20 | | | | |
| 21 | | | | |
| 22 | | | | |
| 23 | | | | |
| 24 | | | | |
| 25 | | | | |
| 26 | | | | |
| 27 | | | | |
| 28 | | | | |
| 29 | | | | |
| 30 | | | | |
| 31 | | | | |
| 32 | | | | |
| 33 | | | | |
| 34 | | | | |
| 35 | | | | |
| 36 | | | | |
| 37 | | | | |
| 38 | | | | |
| 39 | | | | |
| 40 | | | | |
| 41 | | | | |
| 42 | | | | |

**PROBLEM 17-4 ___ , Continued**

| | A | B | C | D |
|---|---|---|---|---|
| 1 | | Costs | | |
| 2 | COSTS | Direct Materials | Conversion | Total |
| 3 | | | | |
| 4 | | | | |
| 5 | | | | |
| 6 | | | | |
| 7 | | | | |
| 8 | | | | |
| 9 | | | | |
| 10 | | | | |
| 11 | | | | |
| 12 | | | | |
| 13 | | | | |
| 14 | | | | |
| 15 | | | | |
| 16 | | | | |
| 17 | | | | |
| 18 | | | | |
| 19 | | | | |
| 20 | | | | |
| 21 | | | | |
| 22 | | | | |
| 23 | | | | |
| 24 | | | | |
| 25 | | | | |
| 26 | | | | |
| 27 | | | | |
| 28 | | | | |
| 29 | | | | |
| 30 | | | | |
| 31 | | | | |
| 32 | | | | |
| 33 | | | | |
| 34 | | | | |
| 35 | | | | |
| 36 | | | | |
| 37 | | | | |
| 38 | | | | |
| 39 | | | | |
| 40 | | | | |
| 41 | | | | |
| 42 | | | | |

**PROBLEM 17-4 ___, Concluded**

3. _____

_____

_____

_____

_____

_____

_____

_____

**APPENDIX PROBLEM 17-5 ___**

|   | A | B | C |
|---|---|---|---|
| 1 | | | |
| 2 | Cost of Production Report—_____ | | |
| 3 | | | |
| 4 | UNITS | Whole Units | Equivalent Units of Production |
| 5 | | | |
| 6 | | | |
| 7 | | | |
| 8 | | | |
| 9 | | | |
| 10 | | | |
| 11 | | | |
| 12 | | | |
| 13 | | | |
| 14 | | | |
| 15 | | | |
| 16 | | | |
| 17 | | | |
| 18 | | | |
| 19 | | | |
| 20 | | | |
| 21 | | | |
| 22 | | | |
| 23 | | | |
| 24 | | | |
| 25 | | | |
| 26 | | | |
| 27 | | | |
| 28 | | | |
| 29 | | | |
| 30 | | | |
| 31 | | | |
| 32 | | | |
| 33 | | | |
| 34 | | | |
| 35 | | | |
| 36 | | | |
| 37 | | | |
| 38 | | | |
| 39 | | | |
| 40 | | | |
| 41 | | | |
| 42 | | | |

**APPENDIX PROBLEM 17-5 ___ , Concluded**

| | A | B |
|---|---|---|
| 1 | COSTS | Costs |
| 2 | | |
| 3 | | |
| 4 | | |
| 5 | | |
| 6 | | |
| 7 | | |
| 8 | | |
| 9 | | |
| 10 | | |
| 11 | | |
| 12 | | |
| 13 | | |
| 14 | | |
| 15 | | |
| 16 | | |
| 17 | | |
| 18 | | |
| 19 | | |
| 20 | | |
| 21 | | |
| 22 | | |
| 23 | | |
| 24 | | |
| 25 | | |
| 26 | | |
| 27 | | |
| 28 | | |
| 29 | | |
| 30 | | |
| 31 | | |
| 32 | | |
| 33 | | |
| 34 | | |
| 35 | | |
| 36 | | |
| 37 | | |
| 38 | | |
| 39 | | |
| 40 | | |
| 41 | | |
| 42 | | |

## EXERCISE 18-1

_____

_____

## EXERCISE 18-2

**A.** _____

     _____

     _____

     _____

     _____

Supporting calculations:

|  |  |  |  |  |  |
|---|---|---|---|---|---|
|  |  |  |  |  |  |
|  |  |  |  |  |  |
|  |  |  |  |  |  |
|  |  |  |  |  |  |
|  |  |  |  |  |  |

**B.**

|  |  |  |  |  |
|---|---|---|---|---|
|  |  |  |  |  |
|  |  |  |  |  |
|  |  |  |  |  |
|  |  |  |  |  |
|  |  |  |  |  |
|  |  |  |  |  |
|  |  |  |  |  |
|  |  |  |  |  |
|  |  |  |  |  |

**EXERCISE 18-3**

A. _____

_____

_____

_____

_____

Supporting calculations:

| | | | |
|---|---|---|---|
| | | | |
| | | | |
| | | | |
| | | | |
| | | | |

B.

| | | | |
|---|---|---|---|
| | | | |
| | | | |
| | | | |
| | | | |
| | | | |
| | | | |
| | | | |
| | | | |
| | | | |

**EXERCISE 18-4**

**A.**

| | | | | |
|---|---|---|---|---|
| | | | | |
| | | | | |
| | | | | |
| | | | | |

_____

_____

_____

_____

_____

**B.**

| | | | |
|---|---|---|---|
| | | | |
| | | | |
| | | | |
| | | | |

**EXERCISE 18-4, Continued**

**C.**

*Product Line Budgeted Gross Profit Reports*

| | PISTONS | VALVES | CAMS |
|---|---|---|---|
| | | | |
| | | | |
| | | | |
| | | | |
| | | | |
| | | | |
| | | | |
| | | | |
| | | | |
| | | | |
| | | | |
| | | | |
| | | | |
| | | | |
| | | | |
| | | | |
| | | | |
| | | | |
| | | | |
| | | | |
| | | | |
| | | | |
| | | | |
| | | | |
| | | | |
| | | | |
| | | | |
| | | | |
| | | | |

**EXERCISE 18-4, Concluded**

**D.** _____

_____

_____

_____

_____

**EXERCISE 18-5**

**A.**

|  | PATTERN DEPARTMENT | CUT AND SEW DEPARTMENT |  |
|---|---|---|---|
|  |  |  |  |
|  |  |  |  |
|  |  |  |  |

**B.** Small Glove:

|  |  |  |  |
|---|---|---|---|
|  |  |  |  |
|  |  |  |  |
|  |  |  |  |
|  |  |  |  |
|  |  |  |  |

Medium Glove:

|  |  |  |  |
|---|---|---|---|
|  |  |  |  |
|  |  |  |  |
|  |  |  |  |
|  |  |  |  |
|  |  |  |  |

Large Glove:

|  |  |  |  |
|---|---|---|---|
|  |  |  |  |
|  |  |  |  |
|  |  |  |  |
|  |  |  |  |

**EXERCISE 18-6**

**A.** _____

_____

_____

_____

_____

|  |  |  |
|---|---|---|
|  |  |  |
|  |  |  |
|  |  |  |
|  |  |  |

**B.**

|  | ASSEMBLY DEPARTMENT | TESTING DEPARTMENT |
|---|---|---|
|  |  |  |
|  |  |  |
|  |  |  |
|  |  |  |

Commercial Motor:

|  |  |  |
|---|---|---|
|  |  |  |
|  |  |  |
|  |  |  |
|  |  |  |

Residential Motor:

|  |  |  |
|---|---|---|
|  |  |  |
|  |  |  |
|  |  |  |
|  |  |  |

**EXERCISE 18-6, Concluded**

C. _____

_____

_____

_____

_____

_____

_____

_____

_____

_____

_____

_____

_____

_____

_____

_____

_____

**EXERCISE 18-7**

A. _____

_____

_____

_____

_____

| | | |
|---|---|---|
| | | |
| | | |
| | | |
| | | |

**EXERCISE 18-7, Continued**

**B.**

| | FABRICATION DEPARTMENT | ASSEMBLY DEPARTMENT | |
|---|---|---|---|
| | | | |
| | | | |
| | | | |
| | | | |
| | | | |

Gasoline Engine:

| | | | |
|---|---|---|---|
| | | | |
| | | | |
| | | | |
| | | | |
| | | | |

Diesel Engine:

| | | | |
|---|---|---|---|
| | | | |
| | | | |
| | | | |
| | | | |
| | | | |

**EXERCISE 18-7, Concluded**

C. _____

_____

_____

_____

_____

_____

_____

_____

_____

_____

_____

_____

_____

_____

_____

_____

_____

_____

_____

_____

_____

_____

## EXERCISE 18-8

| Activity | Activity Base |
|----------|---------------|
| Accounting reports ........................................ | _____ |
| Customer return processing......................... | _____ |
| Electric power............................................... | _____ |
| Human resources.......................................... | _____ |
| Inventory control.......................................... | _____ |
| Invoice and collecting................................. | _____ |
| Machine depreciation .................................. | _____ |
| Materials handling ....................................... | _____ |
| Order shipping.............................................. | _____ |
| Payroll .......................................................... | _____ |
| Production control ....................................... | _____ |
| Production setup .......................................... | _____ |
| Purchasing ................................................... | _____ |
| Quality control ............................................. | _____ |
| Sales order processing ............................... | _____ |

## EXERCISE 18-9

**A.** Sales order processing activity rate: _____

_____

**B.** Sales order processing cost: _____

_____

**EXERCISE 18-10**

| | A | B | C | D | E | F | G | H | I | J | K |
|---|---|---|---|---|---|---|---|---|---|---|---|
| | | | Elliptical Machines | | | | | | Treadmills | | |
| 1 | | | | | | | | | | | |
| 2 | | | | | | | | | | | |
| 3 | | | | | | | | | | | |
| 4 | | | | | | | | | | | |
| 5 | | | | | | | | | | | |
| 6 | | | | | | | | | | | |
| 7 | | | | | | | | | | | |
| 8 | | | | | | | | | | | |
| 9 | | | | | | | | | | | |
| 10 | | | | | | | | | | | |
| 11 | | | | | | | | | | | |
| 12 | | | | | | | | | | | |
| 13 | | | | | | | | | | | |
| 14 | | | | | | | | | | | |
| 15 | | | | | | | | | | | |

**EXERCISE 18-11**

**A.**

|   | A | B | C | D | E | F |
|---|---|---|---|---|---|---|
| 1 |   |   |   |   |   |   |
| 2 |   |   |   |   |   |   |
| 3 |   |   |   |   |   |   |
| 4 |   |   |   |   |   |   |
| 5 |   |   |   |   |   |   |
| 6 |   |   |   |   |   |   |
| 7 |   |   |   |   |   |   |
| 8 |   |   |   |   |   |   |

**EXERCISE 18-11, Concluded**

**B.**

| | A | B | C | D | E | F | G | H | I | J | K |
|---|---|---|---|---|---|---|---|---|---|---|---|
| | | | Entry Lighting Fixtures | | | | | Dining Room Lighting Fixtures | | | |
| 1 | | | | | | | | | | | |
| 2 | | | | | | | | | | | |
| 3 | | | | | | | | | | | |
| 4 | | | | | | | | | | | |
| 5 | | | | | | | | | | | |
| 6 | | | | | | | | | | | |
| 7 | | | | | | | | | | | |
| 8 | | | | | | | | | | | |
| 9 | | | | | | | | | | | |
| 10 | | | | | | | | | | | |
| 11 | | | | | | | | | | | |
| 12 | | | | | | | | | | | |
| 13 | | | | | | | | | | | |
| 14 | | | | | | | | | | | |
| 15 | | | | | | | | | | | |

**EXERCISE 18-12**

**A.**

| | A | B | C | D | E |
|---|---|---|---|---|---|
| 1 | | Procurement | Scheduling | Materials Handling | Product Development |
| 2 | | | | | |
| 3 | | | | | |
| 4 | | | | | |
| 5 | | | | | |

**EXERCISE 18-12, Concluded**

**B.**

| | A | B | C | D | E | F | | G | H | I | J | K |
|---|---|---|---|---|---|---|---|---|---|---|---|---|
| | | | | **Ovens** | | | | **Refrigerators** | | | | |
| 1 | | | | | | | | | | | | |
| 2 | | | | | | | | | | | | |
| 3 | | | | | | | | | | | | |
| 4 | | | | | | | | | | | | |
| 5 | | | | | | | | | | | | |
| 6 | | | | | | | | | | | | |
| 7 | | | | | | | | | | | | |
| 8 | | | | | | | | | | | | |
| 9 | | | | | | | | | | | | |
| 10 | | | | | | | | | | | | |
| 11 | | | | | | | | | | | | |
| 12 | | | | | | | | | | | | |
| 13 | | | | | | | | | | | | |
| 14 | | | | | | | | | | | | |
| 15 | | | | | | | | | | | | |

**EXERCISE 18-13**

A. _____

_____

_____

_____

_____

|  |  |  |  |  |  |  |
|---|---|---|---|---|---|---|
|  |  |  |  |  |  |  |
|  |  |  |  |  |  |  |
|  |  |  |  |  |  |  |
|  |  |  |  |  |  |  |

B.

|  | SETUP | PRODUCTION SUPPORT |  |
|---|---|---|---|
|  |  |  |  |
|  |  |  |  |
|  |  |  |  |
|  |  |  |  |
|  |  |  |  |
|  |  |  |  |
|  |  |  |  |
|  |  |  |  |

**EXERCISE 18-13, Continued**

C.

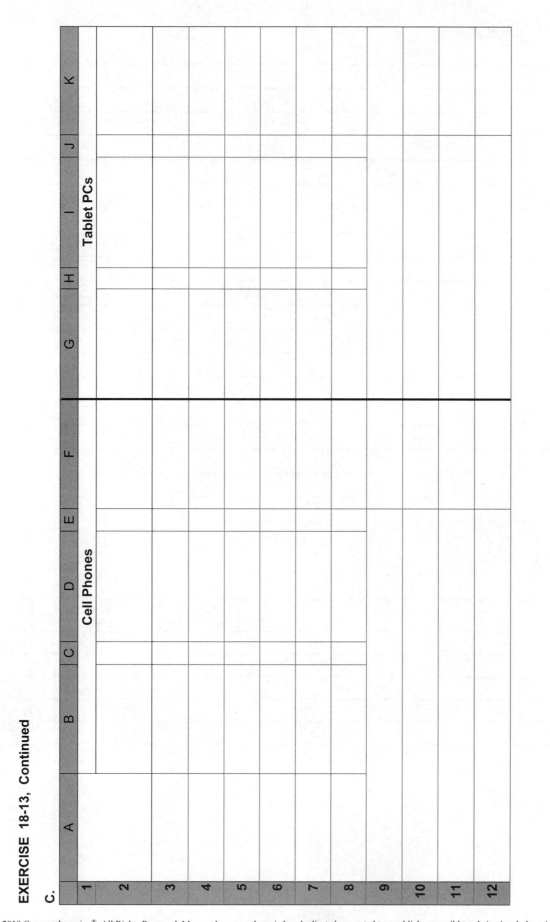

| | A | B | C | D | E | F | G | H | I | J | K |
|---|---|---|---|---|---|---|---|---|---|---|---|
| | | | | Cell Phones | | | | | Tablet PCs | | |
| 1 | | | | | | | | | | | |
| 2 | | | | | | | | | | | |
| 3 | | | | | | | | | | | |
| 4 | | | | | | | | | | | |
| 5 | | | | | | | | | | | |
| 6 | | | | | | | | | | | |
| 7 | | | | | | | | | | | |
| 8 | | | | | | | | | | | |
| 9 | | | | | | | | | | | |
| 10 | | | | | | | | | | | |
| 11 | | | | | | | | | | | |
| 12 | | | | | | | | | | | |

**EXERCISE 18-13, Concluded**

**D.** _____

_____

_____

_____

_____

_____

_____

_____

_____

_____

_____

_____

_____

_____

_____

_____

_____

_____

_____

_____

**EXERCISE 18-14**

**A.**

|  | ASSEMBLY DEPARTMENT | TEST AND PACK DEPARTMENT |  |
|---|---|---|---|
|  |  |  |  |
|  |  |  |  |
|  |  |  |  |
|  |  |  |  |
|  |  |  |  |

**EXERCISE 18-14, Concluded**

**B.**

**EXERCISE 18-15**

**A.**

|  | ASSEMBLY ACTIVITY | TEST AND PACK ACTIVITY | SETUP ACTIVITY |
|---|---|---|---|
|  |  |  |  |
|  |  |  |  |
|  |  |  |  |
|  |  |  |  |
|  |  |  |  |
|  |  |  |  |
|  |  |  |  |
|  |  |  |  |

**EXERCISE 18-15, Concluded**

**B.**

**EXERCISE 18-16**

**A.**

| Product Volume Class | Column A<br>Single Rate Overhead Allocation per Unit | Column B<br>ABC Overhead Allocation per Unit | Column C<br>Percent Change in Allocation<br>(Col. B – Col. A) ÷ Col. A |
|---|---|---|---|
| Low | | | |
| Medium | | | |
| High | | | |

Calculations:

_____

_____

_____

_____

_____

_____

_____

_____

_____

_____

_____

_____

_____

**B.** _____

_____

_____

_____

_____

_____

_____

_____

_____

_____

_____

_____

_____

**EXERCISE 18-16, Concluded**

C. _____

_____

_____

_____

_____

_____

_____

_____

_____

_____

_____

_____

_____

_____

_____

_____

_____

_____

_____

_____

_____

_____

**EXERCISE 18-17**

_____
_____
_____
_____
_____
_____
_____
_____
_____
_____
_____
_____
_____
_____
_____
_____
_____
_____

**EXERCISE 18-18**

**A.** Sales order processing activities:

|  |  |  |  |  |  |
|---|---|---|---|---|---|
|  |  |  |  |  |  |
|  |  |  |  |  |  |
|  |  |  |  |  |  |
|  |  |  |  |  |  |

Post-sale customer service activities:

|  |  |  |  |  |  |
|---|---|---|---|---|---|
|  |  |  |  |  |  |
|  |  |  |  |  |  |
|  |  |  |  |  |  |
|  |  |  |  |  |  |

**EXERCISE 18-18, Continued**

**B.**

| | Product Profitability Report | | |
|---|---|---|---|
| | GENERATORS | AIR COMPRESSORS | TOTAL |
| | | | |
| | | | |
| | | | |
| | | | |
| | | | |
| | | | |
| | | | |
| | | | |
| | | | |
| | | | |
| | | | |
| | | | |
| | | | |
| | | | |
| | | | |
| | | | |
| | | | |
| | | | |
| | | | |
| | | | |
| | | | |
| | | | |
| | | | |
| | | | |
| | | | |
| | | | |
| | | | |
| | | | |
| | | | |
| | | | |

**EXERCISE 18-18, Concluded**

C. _____

_____

_____

_____

_____

_____

_____

_____

_____

_____

_____

_____

_____

_____

_____

_____

_____

**EXERCISE 18-19**

A.

| | Customer Profitability Report | | |
|---|---|---|---|
| | *(assumed data)* | | |
| | CUSTOMER 1 | CUSTOMER 2 | CUSTOMER 3 |
| | | | |
| | | | |
| | | | |
| | | | |
| | | | |
| | | | |
| | | | |
| | | | |
| | | | |
| | | | |
| | | | |
| | | | |
| | | | |
| | | | |
| | | | |
| | | | |
| | | | |
| | | | |
| | | | |
| | | | |
| | | | |
| | | | |
| | | | |
| | | | |
| | | | |
| | | | |
| | | | |
| | | | |
| | | | |

**EXERCISE 18-19, Concluded**

**B.** _____

_____

_____

_____

_____

_____

_____

_____

_____

_____

_____

_____

_____

_____

**EXERCISE 18-20**

**A.**

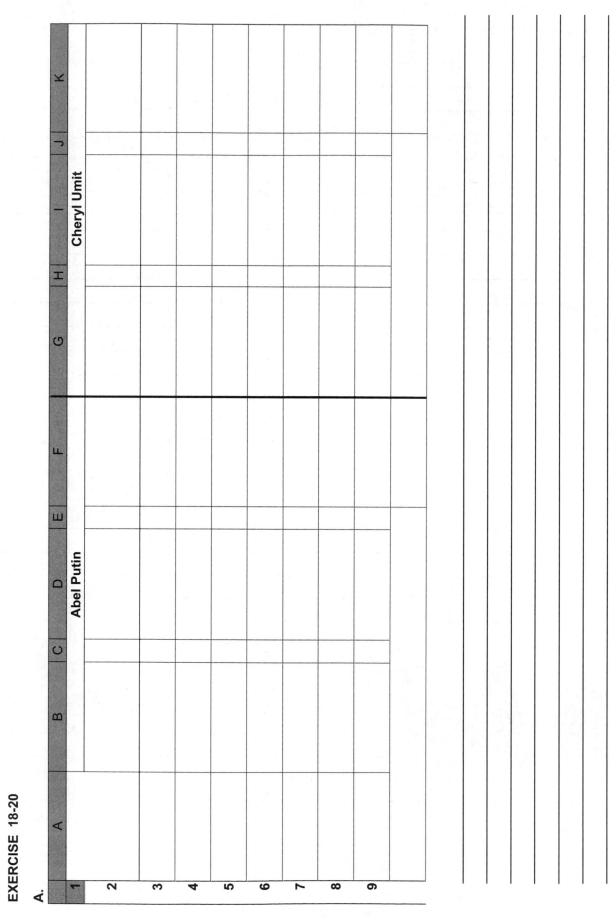

**EXERCISE 18-21**

**A.**

|  | | AUTO | WORKERS' COMPENSATION | HOMEOWNERS | |
|---|---|---|---|---|---|
|  | | | | | |
|  | | | | | |
|  | | | | | |
|  | | | | | |
|  | | | | | |
|  | | | | | |
|  | | | | | |
|  | | | | | |
|  | | | | | |
|  | | | | | |
|  | | | | | |
|  | | | | | |
|  | | | | | |
|  | | | | | |
|  | | | | | |
|  | | | | | |
|  | | | | | |
|  | | | | | |
|  | | | | | |
|  | | | | | |
|  | | | | | |
|  | | | | | |
|  | | | | | |
|  | | | | | |
|  | | | | | |

*Product Profitability Report*

**EXERCISE 18-21, Concluded**

B. _____

_____

_____

_____

_____

_____

_____

_____

_____

_____

_____

_____

_____

_____

_____

_____

_____

_____

_____

_____

**PROBLEM 18-1 ___**

1. **A.** Using direct labor hours: _____

   _____

   _____

   _____

   _____

   **B.** Using machine hours: _____

   _____

   _____

   _____

   _____

2. **A.** Using the direct labor hour plantwide factory overhead rate:

| | | | |
|---|---|---|---|
| | | | |
| | | | |
| | | | |
| | | | |
| | | | |
| | | | |
| | | | |
| | | | |
| | | | |
| | | | |
| | | | |

   **B.** Using the machine hour plantwide factory overhead rate:

| | | | |
|---|---|---|---|
| | | | |
| | | | |
| | | | |
| | | | |
| | | | |
| | | | |
| | | | |
| | | | |

**This Page Not Used.**

**PROBLEM 18-2 \_\_\_**

**1.**

|  | DEPARTMENT | DEPARTMENT |
|---|---|---|
|  |  |  |
|  |  |  |
|  |  |  |
|  |  |  |
|  |  |  |

**2.** _____

|  |  |  |
|---|---|---|
|  |  |  |
|  |  |  |
|  |  |  |
|  |  |  |

|  |  |  |
|---|---|---|
|  |  |  |
|  |  |  |
|  |  |  |
|  |  |  |

|  |  |  |
|---|---|---|
|  |  |  |
|  |  |  |
|  |  |  |
|  |  |  |

**This Page Not Used.**

**PROBLEM 18-3 ___**

**1.**

| | DEPARTMENT | DEPARTMENT |
|---|---|---|
| | | |
| | | |
| | | |
| | | |
| | | |

**2.**

| | | | | |
|---|---|---|---|---|
| | | | | |
| | | | | |
| | | | | |
| | | | | |
| | | | | |
| | | | | |
| | | | | |
| | | | | |
| | | | | |
| | | | | |
| | | | | |
| | | | | |
| | | | | |
| | | | | |
| | | | | |
| | | | | |
| | | | | |
| | | | | |
| | | | | |
| | | | | |
| | | | | |
| | | | | |

**PROBLEM 18-3 ___, Continued**

3.

| | | | | |
|---|---|---|---|---|
| | | | | |
| | | | | |
| | | | | |
| | | | | |
| | | | | |

**PROBLEM 18-3 ____, Continued**

4.

**PROBLEM 18-3 \_\_\_, Concluded**

5. _____

_____

_____

_____

_____

_____

_____

_____

_____

_____

_____

_____

_____

_____

_____

_____

_____

_____

**PROBLEM 18-4** ___

**1.**

**PROBLEM 18-4 ____, Continued**

2.

| | A | B | C | D | E | F | G | H | I | J | K |
|---|---|---|---|---|---|---|---|---|---|---|---|
| 1 | | | | | | | | | | | |
| 2 | | | | | | | | | | | |
| 3 | | | | | | | | | | | |
| 4 | | | | | | | | | | | |
| 5 | | | | | | | | | | | |
| 6 | | | | | | | | | | | |
| 7 | | | | | | | | | | | |
| 8 | | | | | | | | | | | |
| 9 | | | | | | | | | | | |

**PROBLEM 18-4 ___, Concluded**

|   | A | B | C | D | E | F |
|---|---|---|---|---|---|---|
| 1 |   |   |   |   |   |   |
| 2 |   |   |   |   |   |   |
| 3 |   |   |   |   |   |   |
| 4 |   |   |   |   |   |   |
| 5 |   |   |   |   |   |   |
| 6 |   |   |   |   |   |   |
| 7 |   |   |   |   |   |   |
| 8 |   |   |   |   |   |   |
| 9 |   |   |   |   |   |   |
| 10 |   |   |   |   |   |   |
| 11 |   |   |   |   |   |   |
| 12 |   |   |   |   |   |   |
| 13 |   |   |   |   |   |   |
| 14 |   |   |   |   |   |   |
| 15 |   |   |   |   |   |   |

3. _____

_____

_____

_____

_____

_____

_____

_____

_____

_____

**This Page Not Used.**

**PROBLEM 18-5 ___**

**1.**

|  |  |  |  |
|--|--|--|--|
|  |  |  |  |
|  |  |  |  |
|  |  |  |  |
|  |  |  |  |
|  |  |  |  |

**2.** _____

|  |  |  |
|--|--|--|
|  |  |  |
|  |  |  |
|  |  |  |
|  |  |  |

_____

|  |  |  |
|--|--|--|
|  |  |  |
|  |  |  |
|  |  |  |
|  |  |  |

_____

|  |  |  |
|--|--|--|
|  |  |  |
|  |  |  |
|  |  |  |
|  |  |  |

**PROBLEM 18-5 ___, Continued**

3.

| Customer Profitability Report | | | |
|---|---|---|---|
| | | | |
| | | | |
| | | | |
| | | | |
| | | | |
| | | | |
| | | | |
| | | | |
| | | | |
| | | | |
| | | | |
| | | | |
| | | | |
| | | | |
| | | | |
| | | | |
| | | | |
| | | | |
| | | | |
| | | | |
| | | | |

**PROBLEM 18-5 ___, Concluded**

4. _____

_____

_____

_____

_____

_____

_____

_____

_____

_____

_____

_____

_____

_____

_____

_____

_____

_____

_____

_____

_____

_____

_____

_____

_____

_____

_____

_____

_____

_____

_____

_____

_____

_____

_____

_____

This Page Not Used.

**PROBLEM 18-6 ___**

1.

| | | | | |
|---|---|---|---|---|
| | | | | |
| | | | | |
| | | | | |
| | | | | |
| | | | | |
| | | | | |
| | | | | |

_____

_____

_____

_____

_____

_____

_____

**PROBLEM 18-6 ___, Continued**

2.

| | | | | | |
|---|---|---|---|---|---|
| | | | | | |
| | | | | | |
| | | | | | |
| | | | | | |
| | | | | | |
| | | | | | |
| | | | | | |
| | | | | | |
| | | | | | |
| | | | | | |
| | | | | | |
| | | | | | |
| | | | | | |
| | | | | | |
| | | | | | |
| | | | | | |
| | | | | | |
| | | | | | |
| | | | | | |
| | | | | | |
| | | | | | |
| | | | | | |
| | | | | | |

**PROBLEM 18-6 ___, Continued**

3.

_____

_____

| | | | |
|---|---|---|---|
| | | | |
| | | | |
| | | | |
| | | | |
| | | | |
| | | | |
| | | | |
| | | | |
| | | | |
| | | | |
| | | | |
| | | | |
| | | | |
| | | | |
| | | | |
| | | | |
| | | | |
| | | | |
| | | | |

**PROBLEM 18-6 \_\_\_, Concluded**

4. _____

_____

_____

_____

_____

_____

_____

_____

_____

_____

_____

_____

_____

_____

_____

_____

_____

_____

_____

_____

_____

_____

_____

_____

_____

_____

## EXERCISE 19-1

1. _____
2. _____
3. _____
4. _____
5. _____
6. _____
7. _____
8. _____

9. _____
10. _____
11. _____
12. _____
13. _____
14. _____
15. _____

## EXERCISE 19-2

A. _____
B. _____
C. _____

D. _____
E. _____

## EXERCISE 19-3

1. Financial aid office salaries: _____
2. Office supplies: _____
3. Instructor salaries: _____
4. Housing personnel wages: _____
5. Employee wages for maintaining student records: _____
6. Admissions office salaries: _____

## EXERCISE 19-4

1. Preparation costs for each car received: _____
2. Salespersons' commission of 5% of the sales price for each car sold: _____
3. Administrative costs for ordering cars: _____

## EXERCISE 19-5

A. _____
B. _____
C. _____
D. _____
E. _____
F. _____

G. _____
H. _____
I. _____
J. _____
K. _____

**EXERCISE 19-6**

| Memory chips produced............ | 45,000 | | 60,000 | | 75,000 | |
|---|---|---|---|---|---|---|
| **Total costs:** | | | | | | |
| Total variable costs................ | $1,350,000 | (D) _____ | | (J) _____ | | |
| Total fixed costs.................... | 810,000 | (E) _____ | | (K) _____ | | |
| Total costs............................. | $2,160,000 | (F) _____ | | (L) _____ | | |
| **Cost per unit:** | | | | | | |
| Variable cost per unit............. | (A) _____ | (G) _____ | | (M) _____ | | |
| Fixed cost per unit ................. | (B) _____ | (H) _____ | | (N) _____ | | |
| Total cost per unit ................. | (C) _____ | (I) _____ | | (O) _____ | | |

Supporting calculations:

_____

_____

_____

_____

_____

_____

_____

_____

_____

_____

_____

_____

_____

_____

_____

_____

_____

_____

_____

_____

_____

_____

_____

_____

**EXERCISE 19-7**

**A.** Variable Cost per Unit: _____

_____

_____

_____

_____

_____

_____

_____

Fixed Cost: _____

_____

_____

_____

_____

_____

_____

_____

_____

_____

_____

_____

_____

_____

_____

_____

**B.** _____

_____

|  |  |  |
|---|---|---|
|  |  |  |
|  |  |  |
|  |  |  |
|  |  |  |
|  |  |  |

**EXERCISE 19-8**

Variable Cost per Gross-Ton Mile: _____

_____

_____

_____

_____

_____

_____

_____

_____

_____

Fixed Cost: _____

_____

_____

_____

_____

_____

_____

_____

_____

_____

_____

_____

_____

_____

_____

_____

**EXERCISE 19-9**

**A.**

**B.**

**EXERCISE 19-10**

**A.**

**B.**

**EXERCISE 19-10, Concluded**

**C.**

| | | |
|---|---|---|
| | | |
| | | |
| | | |
| | | |

**EXERCISE 19-11**

**A.** _____

_____

_____

_____

_____

**B.** _____

_____

_____

_____

_____

_____

_____

**EXERCISE 19-12**

**A.** _____

_____

_____

_____

_____

_____

_____

_____

_____

_____

**EXERCISE 19-12, Concluded**

B. _____

_____

_____

_____

_____

Calculations:

|  |  |  |  |  |
|---|---|---|---|---|
|  |  |  |  |  |
|  |  |  |  |  |
|  |  |  |  |  |
|  |  |  |  |  |
|  |  |  |  |  |

|  |  |  |  |  |
|---|---|---|---|---|
|  |  |  |  |  |
|  |  |  |  |  |
|  |  |  |  |  |
|  |  |  |  |  |
|  |  |  |  |  |

|  |  |  |  |  |
|---|---|---|---|---|
|  |  |  |  |  |
|  |  |  |  |  |
|  |  |  |  |  |
|  |  |  |  |  |
|  |  |  |  |  |

**EXERCISE 19-13**

A. _____

_____

_____

_____

_____

B. _____

_____

_____

_____

_____

**EXERCISE 19-14**

_____

_____

_____

_____

_____

_____

_____

_____

_____

_____

_____

_____

_____

_____

**EXERCISE  19-15**

**EXERCISE 19-16**

A. _____

_____

_____

_____

_____

_____

_____

Calculations:

_____

_____

| | | | |
|---|---|---|---|
| | | | |
| | | | |
| | | | |
| | | | |
| | | | |
| | | | |
| | | | |
| | | | |

| | | | |
|---|---|---|---|
| | | | |
| | | | |
| | | | |
| | | | |
| | | | |
| | | | |
| | | | |
| | | | |
| | | | |
| | | | |

**EXERCISE 19-16, Concluded**

B. _____

_____

_____

_____

_____

_____

_____

_____

_____

_____

_____

_____

_____

_____

**EXERCISE 19-17**

**A.**

**Sales and Costs**

**Units of Sales**

**B.** _____

_____

**C.** _____

_____

_____

_____

_____

**EXERCISE 19-18**

**A.** _____

_____

**B.**

|  |  |  |
|---|---|---|
|  |  |  |
|  |  |  |
|  |  |  |
|  |  |  |
|  |  |  |

**C.**

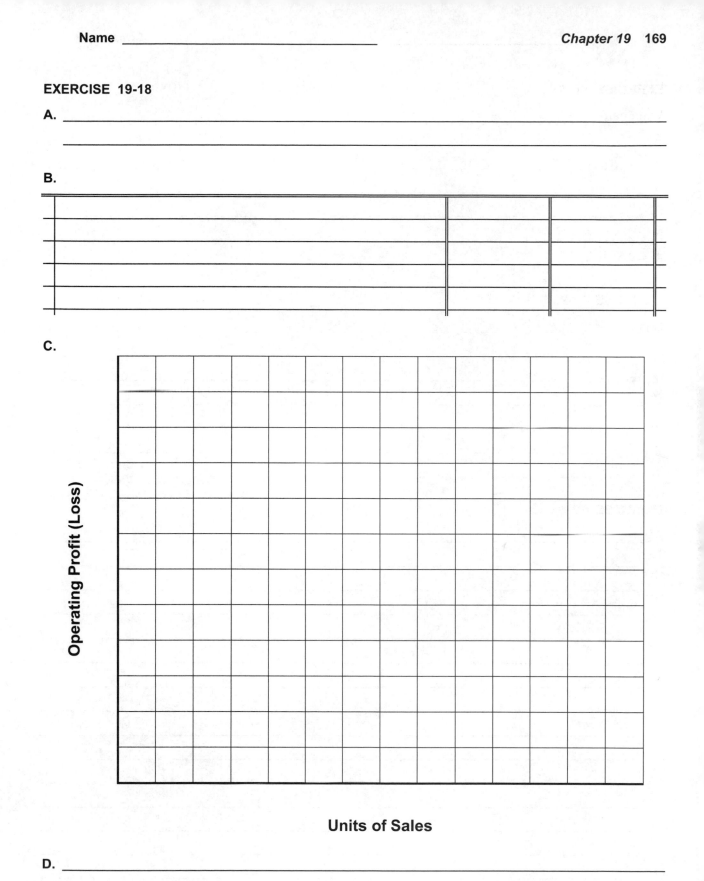

Operating Profit (Loss)

**Units of Sales**

**D.** _____

_____

## EXERCISE 19-19

Chart name: _____

A. _____

B. _____

C. _____

D. _____

E. _____

F. _____

## EXERCISE 19-20

Chart name: _____

A. _____

B. _____

C. _____

D. _____

E. _____

F. _____

## EXERCISE 19-21

A. _____

_____

_____

_____

_____

_____

_____

_____

_____

_____

_____

_____

_____

_____

**B.** Baseball bats: _____

_____

Baseball gloves: _____

_____

**EXERCISE 19-22**

A. _____

_____

_____

_____

_____

_____

_____

Supporting calculations:

| | |
|---|---|
| | |
| | |
| | |
| | |
| | |
| | |
| | |
| | |
| | |
| | |
| | |
| | |
| | |
| | |
| | |
| | |

B.

| | |
|---|---|
| | |
| | |
| | |
| | |
| | |

**EXERCISE 19-23**

**A. (1)** In dollars: _____

_____

_____

_____

_____

**(2)** As a percentage of sales: _____

_____

_____

_____

_____

**B.** _____

_____

_____

_____

_____

_____

_____

_____

_____

_____

_____

_____

_____

_____

_____

_____

_____

_____

_____

_____

**EXERCISE 19-24**

_____

_____

_____

**EXERCISE 19-25**

**A.** Beck Inc.: _____

_____

_____

_____

_____

_____

Bryant Inc.: _____

_____

_____

_____

_____

_____

**B.** _____

_____

_____

_____

_____

_____

**C.** _____

_____

_____

_____

_____

_____

**This Page Not Used.**

**PROBLEM  19-1 ___**

| Cost | Fixed Cost | Variable Cost | Mixed Cost |
|------|------------|---------------|------------|
| A.   |            |               |            |
| B.   |            |               |            |
| C.   |            |               |            |
| D.   |            |               |            |
| E.   |            |               |            |
| F.   |            |               |            |
| G.   |            |               |            |
| H.   |            |               |            |
| I.   |            |               |            |
| J.   |            |               |            |
| K.   |            |               |            |
| L.   |            |               |            |
| M.   |            |               |            |
| N.   |            |               |            |
| O.   |            |               |            |
| P.   |            |               |            |
| Q.   |            |               |            |
| R.   |            |               |            |
| S.   |            |               |            |
| T.   |            |               |            |

**This Page Not Used.**

**PROBLEM 19-2 ___**

1.

| | | | |
|---|---|---|---|
| | | | |
| | | | |
| | | | |
| | | | |
| | | | |

| | | | |
|---|---|---|---|
| | | | |
| | | | |
| | | | |
| | | | |

2.

| | | | |
|---|---|---|---|
| | | | |
| | | | |
| | | | |
| | | | |
| | | | |

**A.** Unit variable cost: _____

_____

**B.** Unit contribution margin: _____

_____

3. _____

_____

_____

_____

_____

_____

_____

**PROBLEM 19-2 ___, Continued**

4. _____

_____

_____

_____

_____

_____

5. _____

_____

_____

_____

_____

_____

_____

_____

_____

_____

_____

6.

|  |  |  |
|---|---|---|
|  |  |  |
|  |  |  |
|  |  |  |
|  |  |  |
|  |  |  |
|  |  |  |

7.

|  |  |
|---|---|
|  |  |
|  |  |
|  |  |
|  |  |

**PROBLEM 19-2 ___, Concluded**

8. _____

_____

_____

_____

_____

_____

_____

_____

_____

_____

_____

_____

_____

_____

_____

_____

_____

_____

_____

_____

_____

_____

_____

This Page Not Used.

**PROBLEM 19-3 ___**

1. _____

_____

_____

_____

_____

_____

_____

_____

_____

_____

2. _____

_____

_____

_____

_____

_____

_____

_____

_____

_____

_____

**PROBLEM 19-3 ___, Concluded**

3.

Sales and Costs

Units of Sales

4.

**PROBLEM 19-4 ___**

1.

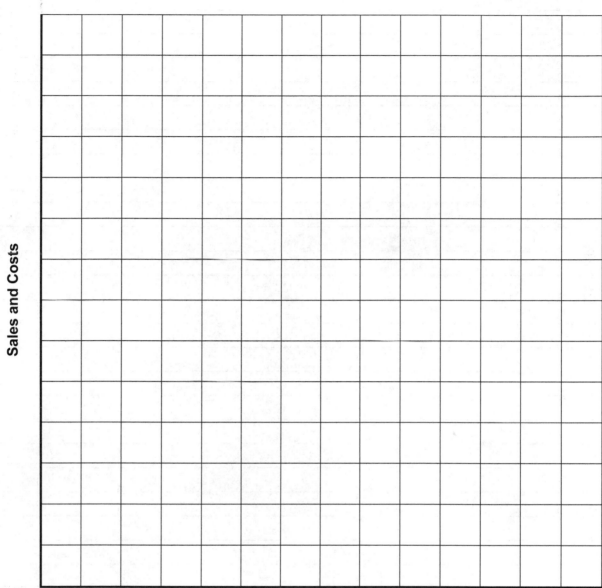

Sales and Costs

Units of Sales

**PROBLEM 19-4 ___, Continued**

**PROBLEM 19-4 ___, Continued**

2.

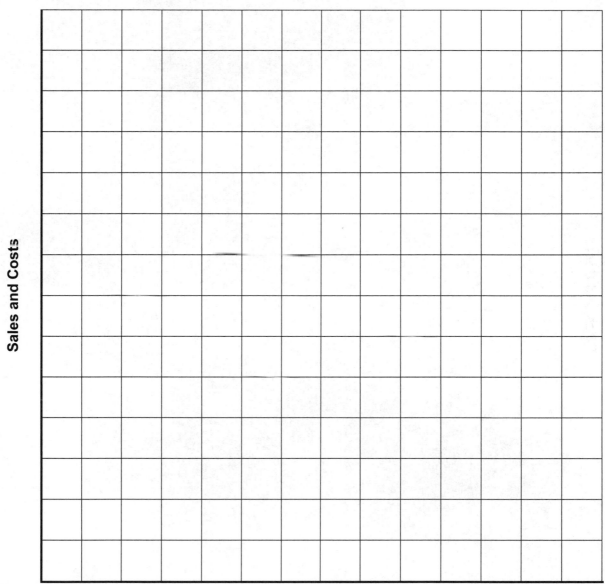

Sales and Costs

Units of Sales

**PROBLEM 19-4 ____,  Continued**

3.

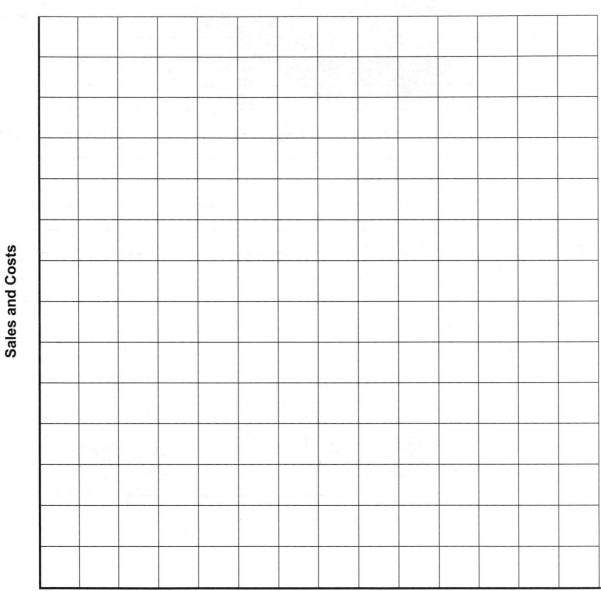

Sales and Costs

Units of Sales

**PROBLEM  19-4 ____ ,  Continued**

_____

_____

_____

_____

_____

_____

_____

_____

_____

_____

_____

_____

_____

_____

_____

_____

_____

_____

_____

_____

_____

_____

_____

_____

_____

_____

_____

_____

_____

_____

_____

_____

_____

_____

**PROBLEM 19-4 ___ , Concluded**

4.

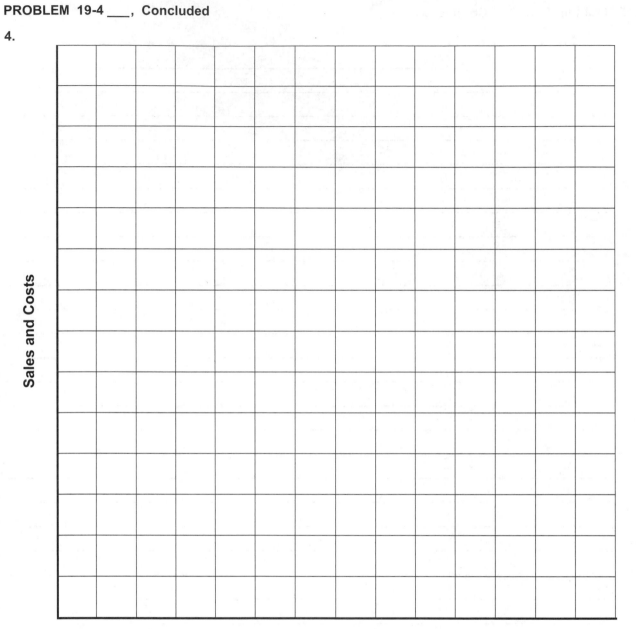

**PROBLEM 19-5 ___**

1.

| | | |
|---|---|---|
| | | |
| | | |
| | | |
| | | |
| | | |

2.

**PROBLEM 19-5 ___, Concluded**

3.

| | | |
|---|---|---|
| | | |
| | | |
| | | |
| | | |
| | | |
| | | |

_____

_____

_____

_____

_____

_____

_____

_____

_____

_____

_____

_____

_____

_____

_____

**PROBLEM 19-6 ___**

1.

| | | | | |
|---|---|---|---|---|
| *Estimated Income Statement* | | | | |
| | | | | |
| | | | | |
| | | | | |
| | | | | |
| | | | | |
| | | | | |
| | | | | |
| | | | | |
| | | | | |
| | | | | |
| | | | | |
| | | | | |
| | | | | |
| | | | | |
| | | | | |
| | | | | |
| | | | | |
| | | | | |
| | | | | |
| | | | | |
| | | | | |
| | | | | |
| | | | | |
| | | | | |
| | | | | |
| | | | | |

**PROBLEM 19-6 ___, Continued**

2. _____

_____

_____

_____

_____

_____

_____

_____

_____

3. _____

_____

_____

_____

_____

_____

_____

_____

_____

_____

_____

_____

_____

_____

_____

_____

_____

**PROBLEM 19-6 ___ , Continued**

4.

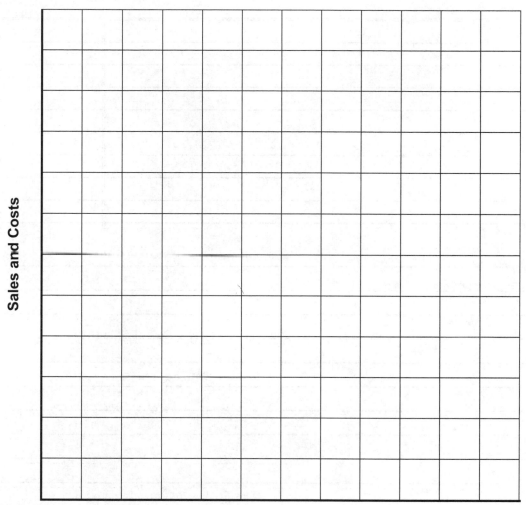

**Sales and Costs** (vertical axis label)

**Units of Sales**

**PROBLEM 19-6 ___, Concluded**

5.

| | | |
|---|---|---|
| | | |
| | | |
| | | |
| | | |
| | | |
| | | |
| | | |
| | | |

_____

_____

_____

_____

_____

_____

_____

_____

_____

_____

6. _____

_____

_____

_____

_____

_____

_____

_____

_____

_____

_____

**EXERCISE 20-1**

**A.** Under the absorption costing concept: _____

_____

_____

_____

_____

|  |  |  |
|---|---|---|
|  |  |  |
|  |  |  |
|  |  |  |
|  |  |  |
|  |  |  |
|  |  |  |

**B.** Under the variable costing concept: _____

_____

_____

_____

|  |  |  |
|---|---|---|
|  |  |  |
|  |  |  |
|  |  |  |
|  |  |  |
|  |  |  |

**EXERCISE 20-2**

**A.**

|  |  |  |
| --- | --- | --- |
| *Absorption Costing Income Statement* | | |

|  |  |  |
| --- | --- | --- |
|  |  |  |
|  |  |  |
|  |  |  |
|  |  |  |
|  |  |  |
|  |  |  |
|  |  |  |

Supporting calculations:

|  |  |  |
| --- | --- | --- |
|  |  |  |
|  |  |  |
|  |  |  |
|  |  |  |
|  |  |  |
|  |  |  |
|  |  |  |
|  |  |  |
|  |  |  |
|  |  |  |

**EXERCISE 20-2, Continued**

**B.**

| | *Variable Costing Income Statement* | | | |
|---|---|---|---|---|
| | | | | |
| | | | | |
| | | | | |
| | | | | |
| | | | | |
| | | | | |
| | | | | |
| | | | | |
| | | | | |
| | | | | |
| | | | | |
| | | | | |
| | | | | |
| | | | | |
| | | | | |
| | | | | |
| | | | | |
| | | | | |
| | | | | |

**EXERCISE 20-3**

**A.**

|  | Absorption Costing Income Statement | | |
|---|---|---|---|
|  |  |  |  |
|  |  |  |  |
|  |  |  |  |
|  |  |  |  |
|  |  |  |  |
|  |  |  |  |
|  |  |  |  |
|  |  |  |  |
|  |  |  |  |
|  |  |  |  |
|  |  |  |  |
|  |  |  |  |
|  |  |  |  |

**B.**

|  | Variable Costing Income Statement | | |
|---|---|---|---|
|  |  |  |  |
|  |  |  |  |
|  |  |  |  |
|  |  |  |  |
|  |  |  |  |
|  |  |  |  |
|  |  |  |  |
|  |  |  |  |
|  |  |  |  |
|  |  |  |  |
|  |  |  |  |
|  |  |  |  |
|  |  |  |  |
|  |  |  |  |
|  |  |  |  |

**EXERCISE 20-3, Concluded**

**C.** _____

_____

_____

_____

_____

_____

_____

_____

_____

_____

_____

_____

_____

_____

_____

_____

_____

_____

_____

|  |  |  |
|---|---|---|
|  |  |  |
|  |  |  |
|  |  |  |
|  |  |  |

**EXERCISE 20-4**

**A.** Variable cost of goods manufactured per unit: _____

_____

_____

_____

_____

_____

_____

_____

**EXERCISE  20-4,  Concluded**

**B.** Absorption cost of goods manufactured per unit: _____

_____

_____

_____

_____

_____

_____

_____

_____

_____

**EXERCISE  20-5**

| *Variable Costing Income Statement* | | |
|---|---|---|
|  |  |  |
|  |  |  |
|  |  |  |
|  |  |  |
|  |  |  |
|  |  |  |
|  |  |  |
|  |  |  |
|  |  |  |
|  |  |  |
|  |  |  |
|  |  |  |
|  |  |  |
|  |  |  |
|  |  |  |
|  |  |  |
|  |  |  |
|  |  |  |
|  |  |  |
|  |  |  |
|  |  |  |
|  |  |  |
|  |  |  |

**EXERCISE 20-6**

| Absorption Costing Income Statement | | |
|---|---|---|
| | | |
| | | |
| | | |
| | | |
| | | |
| | | |
| | | |
| | | |
| | | |
| | | |
| | | |
| | | |
| | | |
| | | |
| | | |
| | | |
| | | |
| | | |
| | | |

**EXERCISE 20-7**

A.

| Variable Costing Income Statement (assumed) | | |
|---|---|---|
| (in millions) | | |
|  |  |  |
|  |  |  |
|  |  |  |
|  |  |  |
|  |  |  |
|  |  |  |
|  |  |  |
|  |  |  |
|  |  |  |
|  |  |  |
|  |  |  |
|  |  |  |
|  |  |  |
|  |  |  |
|  |  |  |
|  |  |  |
|  |  |  |
|  |  |  |
|  |  |  |
|  |  |  |

B. _____

_____

_____

_____

_____

_____

_____

_____

_____

_____

**EXERCISE 20-8**

**A. (1)**

*Absorption Costing Income Statement*

|  | 40,000 UNITS MANUFACTURED | 50,000 UNITS MANUFACTURED |
|---|---|---|
|  |  |  |
|  |  |  |
|  |  |  |
|  |  |  |
|  |  |  |
|  |  |  |
|  |  |  |
|  |  |  |
|  |  |  |
|  |  |  |
|  |  |  |
|  |  |  |
|  |  |  |

Supporting calculations:

|  |  |
|---|---|
|  |  |
|  |  |
|  |  |
|  |  |
|  |  |
|  |  |
|  |  |
|  |  |
|  |  |
|  |  |
|  |  |
|  |  |
|  |  |
|  |  |

**EXERCISE 20-8, Continued**

(2)

| | | | |
|---|---|---|---|
| | | | |
| *Variable Costing Income Statement* | | | |
| | | | |

| | 40,000 UNITS MANUFACTURED | 50,000 UNITS MANUFACTURED | |
|---|---|---|---|
| | | | |
| | | | |
| | | | |
| | | | |
| | | | |
| | | | |
| | | | |
| | | | |
| | | | |
| | | | |
| | | | |
| | | | |
| | | | |
| | | | |
| | | | |
| | | | |
| | | | |
| | | | |
| | | | |
| | | | |
| | | | |
| | | | |
| | | | |
| | | | |
| | | | |
| | | | |

Supporting calculations:

| | | |
|---|---|---|
| | | |
| | | |
| | | |
| | | |
| | | |
| | | |

**EXERCISE 20-8, Concluded**

**B.** _____

_____

_____

_____

_____

_____

_____

_____

_____

_____

_____

_____

_____

_____

_____

_____

_____

**EXERCISE 20-9**

A.

|  | Variable Costing Income Statement (assumed) | | |
|---|---|---|---|
|  | (in millions) | | |
|  |  |  |  |
|  |  |  |  |
|  |  |  |  |
|  |  |  |  |
|  |  |  |  |
|  |  |  |  |
|  |  |  |  |
|  |  |  |  |
|  |  |  |  |
|  |  |  |  |
|  |  |  |  |
|  |  |  |  |
|  |  |  |  |
|  |  |  |  |
|  |  |  |  |
|  |  |  |  |
|  |  |  |  |
|  |  |  |  |
|  |  |  |  |
|  |  |  |  |
|  |  |  |  |
|  |  |  |  |

Supporting calculations:

|  |  |  |
|---|---|---|
|  |  |  |
|  |  |  |
|  |  |  |
|  |  |  |
|  |  |  |
|  |  |  |
|  |  |  |
|  |  |  |
|  |  |  |
|  |  |  |
|  |  |  |
|  |  |  |

**EXERCISE 20-9, Concluded**

B. _____

_____

_____

_____

_____

_____

_____

_____

_____

_____

_____

_____

_____

_____

_____

_____

_____

_____

_____

_____

_____

_____

_____

_____

|  |  |
|---|---|
|  |  |
|  |  |
|  |  |
|  |  |
|  |  |
|  |  |
|  |  |
|  |  |

**EXERCISE 20-10**

**A.** _____

_____

_____

_____

_____

_____

_____

_____

_____

_____

**B.**

*Variable Costing Income Statements—Three Product Lines*

| | CROSS TRAINING SHOES | GOLF SHOES | RUNNING SHOES |
|---|---|---|---|
| | | | |
| | | | |
| | | | |
| | | | |
| | | | |
| | | | |
| | | | |
| | | | |
| | | | |
| | | | |
| | | | |
| | | | |
| | | | |
| | | | |
| | | | |
| | | | |
| | | | |
| | | | |

**EXERCISE 20-10, Concluded**

C. _____

_____

_____

_____

_____

_____

_____

_____

_____

_____

**EXERCISE 20-11**

|  |  |  |
|---|---|---|
|  |  |  |
|  |  |  |
|  |  |  |
|  |  |  |
|  |  |  |

_____

_____

_____

_____

_____

_____

_____

**EXERCISE 20-12**

A.

|  | | Contribution Margin by Product | | |
|---|---|---|---|---|
|  | | MOUNTAIN MONSTER | DESERT DRAGON | |
|  | | | | |
|  | | | | |
|  | | | | |
|  | | | | |
|  | | | | |
|  | | | | |
|  | | | | |
|  | | | | |

B. _____

_____

_____

_____

_____

_____

**EXERCISE 20-13**

A.

|  | | Contribution Margin by Territory | | |
|---|---|---|---|---|
|  | | EAST COAST | WEST COAST | |
|  | | | | |
|  | | | | |
|  | | | | |
|  | | | | |
|  | | | | |
|  | | | | |
|  | | | | |

**EXERCISE 20-13, Concluded**

**B.** _____

_____

_____

_____

_____

_____

_____

_____

_____

_____

_____

_____

_____

_____

_____

_____

_____

_____

_____

_____

_____

_____

_____

**EXERCISE 20-14**

A. 1.

| Contribution Margin by Salesperson | | | | |
|---|---|---|---|---|
| | RENE | STEVE | COLLEEN | PAUL |
| | | | | |
| | | | | |
| | | | | |
| | | | | |
| | | | | |
| | | | | |
| | | | | |
| | | | | |
| | | | | |

2. _____

_____

_____

_____

_____

_____

_____

_____

_____

_____

_____

_____

_____

_____

_____

_____

_____

_____

_____

_____

_____

_____

**EXERCISE 20-14, Concluded**

**B. 1.**

| Contribution Margin by Territory | NORTHEAST | SOUTHWEST | |
|---|---|---|---|
| | | | |
| | | | |
| | | | |
| | | | |
| | | | |
| | | | |
| | | | |
| | | | |
| | | | |

**2.** _____

_____

_____

_____

_____

_____

_____

_____

_____

_____

_____

_____

_____

_____

**EXERCISE 20-15**

**A.**

Contribution Margin by Segment (assumed)

(in millions, except ratio figures)

| | BUILDING CONSTRUCTION PRODUCTS | CAT JAPAN | CORE COMPONENTS | EARTHMOVING | ELECTRIC POWER | EXCAVATION | LARGE POWER SYSTEMS | LOGISTICS | MARINE & PETROLEUM POWER | MINING | TURBINES |
|---|---|---|---|---|---|---|---|---|---|---|---|
| | | | | | | | | | | | |
| | | | | | | | | | | | |
| | | | | | | | | | | | |
| | | | | | | | | | | | |
| | | | | | | | | | | | |
| | | | | | | | | | | | |
| | | | | | | | | | | | |

**EXERCISE 20-15, Continued**

**B.**

| | BUILDING CONSTRUCTION PRODUCTS | CAT JAPAN | CORE COMPONENTS | EARTHMOVING | ELECTRIC POWER | EXCAVATION | LARGE POWER SYSTEMS | LOGISTICS | MARINE & PETROLEUM POWER | MINING | TURBINES |
|---|---|---|---|---|---|---|---|---|---|---|---|
| | | | | | | | | | | | |
| | | | | | | | | | | | |
| | | | | | | | | | | | |
| | | | | | | | | | | | |
| | | | | | | | | | | | |
| | | | | | | | | | | | |
| | | | | | | | | | | | |
| | | | | | | | | | | | |

**EXERCISE 20-15, Concluded**

**C.** _____

_____

_____

_____

_____

_____

_____

_____

_____

_____

_____

_____

_____

_____

_____

_____

_____

_____

_____

_____

_____

_____

_____

_____

**EXERCISE 20-16**

**A.**

| | | TURNER | HOME BOX OFFICE | WARNER BROS. | |
|---|---|---|---|---|---|
| *Contribution Margin by Segment (assumed)* | | | | | |
| *(in millions, except ratio figures)* | | | | | |
| | | | | | |
| | | | | | |
| | | | | | |
| | | | | | |
| | | | | | |

**EXERCISE 20-16, Concluded**

B. _____

_____

_____

_____

_____

_____

_____

_____

_____

_____

_____

_____

_____

_____

**EXERCISE 20-17**

**A.**

|  | Contribution Margin Analysis—Sales |  |  |
|---|---|---|---|
|  |  |  |  |
|  |  |  |  |
|  |  |  |  |
|  |  |  |  |
|  |  |  |  |
|  |  |  |  |
|  |  |  |  |
|  |  |  |  |
|  |  |  |  |
|  |  |  |  |

**B.** _____

_____

_____

_____

_____

_____

_____

_____

_____

**EXERCISE 20-18**

|  | Contribution Margin Analysis—Sales |  |  |
|---|---|---|---|
|  |  |  |  |
|  |  |  |  |
|  |  |  |  |
|  |  |  |  |
|  |  |  |  |
|  |  |  |  |
|  |  |  |  |
|  |  |  |  |
|  |  |  |  |

**EXERCISE 20-19**

*Contribution Margin Analysis—Variable Costs*

| | | |
|---|---|---|
| | | |
| | | |
| | | |
| | | |
| | | |
| | | |
| | | |
| | | |
| | | |
| | | |
| | | |
| | | |
| | | |
| | | |
| | | |
| | | |
| | | |
| | | |
| | | |
| | | |
| | | |
| | | |
| | | |
| | | |
| | | |
| | | |
| | | |

**EXERCISE 20-20**

A.

| | ATLANTA/ BALTIMORE | BALTIMORE/ PITTSBURGH | PITTSBURGH/ ATLANTA | TOTAL | |
|---|---|---|---|---|---|
| | | | | | |
| | | | | | |
| | | | | | |
| | | | | | |
| | | | | | |
| | | | | | |
| | | | | | |
| | | | | | |
| | | | | | |
| | | | | | |
| | | | | | |
| | | | | | |
| | | | | | |
| | | | | | |
| | | | | | |
| | | | | | |

Contribution Margin by Route

**EXERCISE 20-20, Concluded**

B.   _____

   _____

   _____

   _____

   _____

   _____

   _____

   _____

   _____

   _____

   _____

   _____

   _____

   _____

**EXERCISE 20-21**

**A.**

| *Contribution Margin Report for Atlanta/Baltimore Route* | | |
|---|---|---|
| | | |
| | | |
| | | |
| | | |
| | | |
| | | |
| | | |
| | | |
| | | |
| | | |
| | | |
| | | |
| | | |
| | | |
| | | |
| | | |

**EXERCISE 20-21, Concluded**

**B.**

*Contribution Margin Analysis—Atlanta/Baltimore Route*

|  |  |  |
|---|---|---|
|  |  |  |
|  |  |  |
|  |  |  |
|  |  |  |
|  |  |  |
|  |  |  |
|  |  |  |
|  |  |  |
|  |  |  |
|  |  |  |
|  |  |  |
|  |  |  |
|  |  |  |
|  |  |  |
|  |  |  |
|  |  |  |
|  |  |  |
|  |  |  |
|  |  |  |
|  |  |  |
|  |  |  |
|  |  |  |

**EXERCISE 20-22**

**A.**

| | *Variable Costing Income Statement* | | |
|---|---|---|---|
| | | | |
| | | | |
| | | | |
| | | | |
| | | | |
| | | | |
| | | | |
| | | | |
| | | | |

Supporting calculations:

_____

_____

_____

_____

_____

**EXERCISE 20-22, Concluded**

**B.**

| *Contribution Margin Analysis* | | |
|---|---|---|
| | | |
| | | |
| | | |
| | | |
| | | |
| | | |
| | | |
| | | |
| | | |
| | | |
| | | |
| | | |
| | | |
| | | |
| | | |
| | | |
| | | |
| | | |
| | | |
| | | |
| | | |
| | | |
| | | |
| | | |
| | | |
| | | |
| | | |

**PROBLEM 20-1 ___**

1.

| Absorption Costing Income Statement | | | |
|---|---|---|---|
| | | | |
| | | | |
| | | | |
| | | | |
| | | | |
| | | | |
| | | | |
| | | | |
| | | | |
| | | | |
| | | | |
| | | | |
| | | | |

**PROBLEM 20-1 ___, Continued**

2.

| *Variable Costing Income Statement* | | |
|---|---|---|
|  |  |  |
|  |  |  |
|  |  |  |
|  |  |  |
|  |  |  |
|  |  |  |
|  |  |  |
|  |  |  |
|  |  |  |
|  |  |  |
|  |  |  |
|  |  |  |
|  |  |  |
|  |  |  |
|  |  |  |
|  |  |  |
|  |  |  |
|  |  |  |
|  |  |  |
|  |  |  |
|  |  |  |
|  |  |  |
|  |  |  |
|  |  |  |

**PROBLEM 20-1 ___ , Concluded**

3. _____

_____

_____

_____

_____

_____

_____

_____

_____

_____

_____

_____

**This Page Not Used.**

**PROBLEM 20-2 ___**

1.

| _Estimated Income Statement—Absorption Costing—_____ | | |
|---|---|---|
| | | |
| | | |
| | | |
| | | |
| | | |
| | | |
| | | |
| | | |
| | | |
| | | |
| | | |
| | | |
| | | |
| | | |
| | | |
| | | |
| | | |
| | | |

**PROBLEM 20-2 ___, Continued**

2.

|  | *Estimated Income Statement—Variable Costing—*_____ | | |
|---|---|---|---|
|  |  |  |  |
|  |  |  |  |
|  |  |  |  |
|  |  |  |  |
|  |  |  |  |
|  |  |  |  |
|  |  |  |  |
|  |  |  |  |
|  |  |  |  |
|  |  |  |  |
|  |  |  |  |
|  |  |  |  |
|  |  |  |  |
|  |  |  |  |
|  |  |  |  |
|  |  |  |  |
|  |  |  |  |
|  |  |  |  |
|  |  |  |  |
|  |  |  |  |
|  |  |  |  |

**PROBLEM 20-2 ___, Concluded**

3. _____

_____

_____

_____

_____

_____

_____

_____

_____

_____

_____

4. _____

_____

_____

_____

_____

_____

_____

_____

_____

_____

**This Page Not Used.**

**PROBLEM  20-3 ____**

**1. A.**

| Absorption Costing Income Statement | | |
|---|---|---|
|  |  |  |
|  |  |  |
|  |  |  |
|  |  |  |
|  |  |  |
|  |  |  |
|  |  |  |
|  |  |  |
|  |  |  |
|  |  |  |
|  |  |  |
|  |  |  |
|  |  |  |
|  |  |  |
|  |  |  |

**B.**

| Absorption Costing Income Statement | | |
|---|---|---|
|  |  |  |
|  |  |  |
|  |  |  |
|  |  |  |
|  |  |  |
|  |  |  |
|  |  |  |
|  |  |  |
|  |  |  |
|  |  |  |
|  |  |  |

**PROBLEM 20-3 ___, Continued**

**2. A.**

*Variable Costing Income Statement*

| | | |
|---|---|---|
| | | |
| | | |
| | | |
| | | |
| | | |
| | | |
| | | |
| | | |
| | | |
| | | |
| | | |
| | | |
| | | |
| | | |
| | | |
| | | |
| | | |
| | | |
| | | |
| | | |
| | | |
| | | |
| | | |
| | | |
| | | |

**PROBLEM 20-3 ___, Continued**

B.

| Variable Costing Income Statement | | |
|---|---|---|
| | | |
| | | |
| | | |
| | | |
| | | |
| | | |
| | | |
| | | |
| | | |
| | | |
| | | |
| | | |
| | | |
| | | |
| | | |
| | | |
| | | |
| | | |

**PROBLEM 20-3 ___, Concluded**

3. A. _____

_____

_____

_____

_____

_____

_____

_____

_____

_____

_____

B. _____

_____

_____

_____

_____

_____

_____

_____

_____

_____

_____

_____

4. _____

_____

_____

_____

_____

_____

_____

_____

_____

**PROBLEM 20-4 ___**

1.

| | Salespersons' Analysis<br>For the Year Ended _____ | | | |
|---|---|---|---|---|
| Salesperson | Contribution Margin | Variable Cost of Goods Sold as a Percent of Sales | Variable Selling Expenses as a Percent of Sales | Contribution Margin Ratio |
| | | | | |
| | | | | |
| | | | | |
| | | | | |
| | | | | |
| | | | | |
| | | | | |
| | | | | |

2. _____
_____
_____
_____
_____
_____
_____
_____
_____
_____
_____
_____
_____

3. _____
_____
_____
_____
_____
_____
_____

240

This Page Not Used.

**PROBLEM  20-5 ___**

**1.**

|  | Variable Costing Income Statement | | | |
|---|---|---|---|---|
|  | SIZE | | | TOTAL |
|  | S | M | L |  |
|  |  |  |  |  |
|  |  |  |  |  |
|  |  |  |  |  |
|  |  |  |  |  |
|  |  |  |  |  |
|  |  |  |  |  |
|  |  |  |  |  |
|  |  |  |  |  |
|  |  |  |  |  |
|  |  |  |  |  |
|  |  |  |  |  |
|  |  |  |  |  |
|  |  |  |  |  |
|  |  |  |  |  |
|  |  |  |  |  |
|  |  |  |  |  |
|  |  |  |  |  |

**PROBLEM 20-5 ___, Continued**

2. _____

---

| | | |
|---|---|---|
| | | |
| | | |
| | | |
| | | |
| | | |
| | | |

**PROBLEM 20-5 ___, Concluded**

**3.**

| | | | | | |
|---|---|---|---|---|---|

**Variable Costing Income Statement**

| | SIZE | | TOTAL |
|---|---|---|---|
| | S | L | |
| | | | |
| | | | |
| | | | |
| | | | |
| | | | |
| | | | |
| | | | |
| | | | |
| | | | |
| | | | |
| | | | |
| | | | |
| | | | |
| | | | |

**4.** _____

_____

_____

_____

| | | |
|---|---|---|
| | | |
| | | |
| | | |
| | | |
| | | |
| | | |
| | | |
| | | |

**This Page Not Used.**

**PROBLEM 20-6 ___**

1.

| Contribution Margin Analysis | | |
|---|---|---|
|  |  |  |
|  |  |  |
|  |  |  |
|  |  |  |
|  |  |  |
|  |  |  |
|  |  |  |
|  |  |  |
|  |  |  |
|  |  |  |
|  |  |  |
|  |  |  |
|  |  |  |
|  |  |  |
|  |  |  |
|  |  |  |
|  |  |  |
|  |  |  |
|  |  |  |
|  |  |  |
|  |  |  |
|  |  |  |
|  |  |  |
|  |  |  |
|  |  |  |
|  |  |  |

**PROBLEM 20-6 ___, Concluded**

2. _____

_____

_____

_____

_____

_____

_____

_____

_____

_____

_____

_____

_____

_____

_____

_____

_____

_____

_____

_____

_____

_____

_____

_____

_____

_____

_____

_____

_____

**EXERCISE 21-1**

A.

| | A | B | C | D | E |
|---|---|---|---|---|---|
| 1 | | Priscilla Wescott | | | |
| 2 | | Cash Budget | | | |
| 3 | | For the Four Months Ending December 31 | | | |
| 4 | | September | October | November | December |
| 5 | | | | | |
| 6 | | | | | |
| 7 | | | | | |
| 8 | | | | | |
| 9 | | | | | |
| 10 | | | | | |
| 11 | | | | | |
| 12 | | | | | |
| 13 | | | | | |
| 14 | | | | | |
| 15 | | | | | |
| 16 | | | | | |
| 17 | | | | | |
| 18 | | | | | |
| 19 | | | | | |
| 20 | | | | | |
| 21 | | | | | |
| 22 | | | | | |
| 23 | | | | | |
| 24 | | | | | |
| 25 | | | | | |
| 26 | | | | | |
| 27 | | | | | |
| 28 | | | | | |

B. _____

_____

_____

**EXERCISE 21-1, Concluded**

C. _____

_____

_____

_____

_____

_____

_____

_____

_____

_____

_____

_____

_____

_____

_____

_____

_____

_____

_____

_____

_____

_____

**EXERCISE 21-2**

| | A | B | C | D |
|---|---|---|---|---|
| 1 | Cloud Productivity Inc. | | | |
| 2 | Flexible Selling and Administrative Expenses Budget | | | |
| 3 | For the Month Ending March 31 | | | |
| 4 | | | | |
| 5 | | | | |
| 6 | | | | |
| 7 | | | | |
| 8 | | | | |
| 9 | | | | |
| 10 | | | | |
| 11 | | | | |
| 12 | | | | |
| 13 | | | | |
| 14 | | | | |
| 15 | | | | |
| 16 | | | | |
| 17 | | | | |
| 18 | | | | |
| 19 | | | | |
| 20 | | | | |
| 21 | | | | |
| 22 | | | | |
| 23 | | | | |
| 24 | | | | |
| 25 | | | | |
| 26 | | | | |
| 27 | | | | |
| 28 | | | | |

**EXERCISE 21-3**

**A.**

|  | A | B | C | D |
|---|---|---|---|---|
| 1 | Niland Company | | | |
| 2 | Machining Department Budget | | | |
| 3 | For the Three Months Ending March 31 | | | |
| 4 | | January | February | March |
| 5 | | | | |
| 6 | | | | |
| 7 | | | | |
| 8 | | | | |
| 9 | | | | |
| 10 | | | | |
| 11 | | | | |
| 12 | | | | |
| 13 | | | | |
| 14 | | | | |
| 15 | | | | |
| 16 | | | | |
| 17 | | | | |
| 18 | | | | |
| 19 | | | | |
| 20 | | | | |
| 21 | | | | |
| 22 | | | | |
| 23 | | | | |
| 24 | | | | |
| 25 | | | | |

_____

_____

_____

_____

_____

**EXERCISE 21-3, Concluded**

**B.**

|  | JANUARY | FEBRUARY | MARCH |
|---|---|---|---|
|  |  |  |  |
|  |  |  |  |
|  |  |  |  |
|  |  |  |  |

_____
_____
_____
_____
_____
_____
_____
_____
_____
_____
_____

**EXERCISE 21-4**

|  | A | B | C | D |
|---|---|---|---|---|
| 1 | Steelcase Inc. |  |  |  |
| 2 | Assembly Department Budget |  |  |  |
| 3 | For the Month Ending March 31 |  |  |  |
| 4 | (assumed data) |  |  |  |
| 5 |  |  |  |  |
| 6 |  |  |  |  |
| 7 |  |  |  |  |
| 8 |  |  |  |  |
| 9 |  |  |  |  |
| 10 |  |  |  |  |
| 11 |  |  |  |  |
| 12 |  |  |  |  |
| 13 |  |  |  |  |
| 14 |  |  |  |  |
| 15 |  |  |  |  |
| 16 |  |  |  |  |
| 17 |  |  |  |  |
| 18 |  |  |  |  |
| 19 |  |  |  |  |

**EXERCISE 21-5**

|   | A | B | C |
|---|---|---|---|
| 1 | Weightless Inc. | | |
| 2 | Production Budget | | |
| 3 | For the Month Ending October 31 | | |
| 4 | | Units | |
| 5 | | Bath Scale | Gym Scale |
| 6 | | | |
| 7 | | | |
| 8 | | | |
| 9 | | | |
| 10 | | | |
| 11 | | | |
| 12 | | | |
| 13 | | | |
| 14 | | | |

**EXERCISE 21-6**

**A.**

|   | A | B | C | D |
|---|---|---|---|---|
| 1 | Sonic Inc. | | | |
| 2 | Sales Budget | | | |
| 3 | For the Month Ending June 30 | | | |
| 4 | Product and Area | Unit Sales Volume | Unit Selling Price | Total Sales |
| 5 | | | | |
| 6 | | | | |
| 7 | | | | |
| 8 | | | | |
| 9 | | | | |
| 10 | | | | |
| 11 | | | | |
| 12 | | | | |
| 13 | | | | |
| 14 | | | | |

**EXERCISE 21-10**

| | A | B | C | D |
|---|---|---|---|---|
| 1 | Coca-Cola Enterprises—Wakefield Plant | | | |
| 2 | Direct Materials Purchases Budget | | | |
| 3 | For the Month Ending May 31 | | | |
| 4 | (assumed data) | | | |
| 5 | | Concentrate | 2-Liter Bottles | Carbonated Water |
| 6 | | | | |
| 7 | | | | |
| 8 | | | | |
| 9 | | | | |
| 10 | | | | |
| 11 | | | | |
| 12 | | | | |
| 13 | | | | |
| 14 | | | | |
| 15 | | | | |

Supporting calculations:

| | | |
|---|---|---|
| | | |
| | | |
| | | |
| | | |
| | | |
| | | |
| | | |
| | | |
| | | |
| | | |
| | | |

**EXERCISE 21-11**

| | A | B | C | D |
|---|---|---|---|---|
| 1 | Safety Grip Company | | | |
| 2 | Direct Materials Purchases Budget | | | |
| 3 | For the Year Ending December 31, 20Y9 | | | |
| 4 | | Rubber | Steel Belts | Total |
| 5 | | | | |
| 6 | | | | |
| 7 | | | | |
| 8 | | | | |
| 9 | | | | |
| 10 | | | | |
| 11 | | | | |
| 12 | | | | |
| 13 | | | | |
| 14 | | | | |
| 15 | | | | |
| 16 | | | | |
| 17 | | | | |
| 18 | | | | |
| 19 | | | | |
| 20 | | | | |
| 21 | | | | |
| 22 | | | | |
| 23 | | | | |
| 24 | | | | |
| 25 | | | | |
| 26 | | | | |
| 27 | | | | |
| 28 | | | | |

**EXERCISE 21-12**

| | A | B | C |
|---|---|---|---|
| 1 | Ace Racket Company | | |
| 2 | Direct Labor Cost Budget | | |
| 3 | For the Month Ending July 31 | | |
| 4 | | Forming Department | Assembly Department |
| 5 | | | |
| 6 | | | |
| 7 | | | |
| 8 | | | |
| 9 | | | |
| 10 | | | |
| 11 | | | |
| 12 | | | |
| 13 | | | |
| 14 | | | |
| 15 | | | |
| 16 | | | |
| 17 | | | |
| 18 | | | |
| 19 | | | |
| 20 | | | |

**EXERCISE 21-13**

A.

| | A | B | C |
|---|---|---|---|
| 1 | Levi Strauss & Co. | | |
| 2 | Production Budget | | |
| 3 | For the Month Ending May 31 | | |
| 4 | (assumed data) | | |
| 5 | | Dockers® | 501 Jeans® |
| 6 | | | |
| 7 | | | |
| 8 | | | |
| 9 | | | |
| 10 | | | |
| 11 | | | |
| 12 | | | |
| 13 | | | |
| 14 | | | |
| 15 | | | |

**EXERCISE 21-13,  Concluded**

B.

|   | A | Inseam | Outerseam | Pockets | Zipper | Total |
|---|---|---|---|---|---|---|
| 1 | Levi Strauss & Co. | | | | | |
| 2 | Direct Labor Cost Budget | | | | | |
| 3 | For the Month Ending May 31 | | | | | |
| 4 | (assumed data) | | | | | |
| 5 | | Inseam | Outerseam | Pockets | Zipper | Total |
| 6 | | | | | | |
| 7 | | | | | | |
| 8 | | | | | | |
| 9 | | | | | | |
| 10 | | | | | | |
| 11 | | | | | | |
| 12 | | | | | | |
| 13 | | | | | | |
| 14 | | | | | | |
| 15 | | | | | | |
| 16 | | | | | | |
| 17 | | | | | | |
| 18 | | | | | | |
| 19 | | | | | | |
| 20 | | | | | | |
| 21 | | | | | | |
| 22 | | | | | | |
| 23 | | | | | | |
| 24 | | | | | | |
| 25 | | | | | | |
| 26 | | | | | | |
| 27 | | | | | | |
| 28 | | | | | | |
| 29 | | | | | | |
| 30 | | | | | | |
| 31 | | | | | | |
| 32 | | | | | | |

**EXERCISE 21-14**

| | A | B | C |
|---|---|---|---|
| 1 | **Sweet Tooth Candy Company** | | |
| 2 | **Factory Overhead Cost Budget** | | |
| 3 | **For the Month Ending August 31** | | |
| 4 | | | |
| 5 | | | |
| 6 | | | |
| 7 | | | |
| 8 | | | |
| 9 | | | |
| 10 | | | |
| 11 | | | |
| 12 | | | |
| 13 | | | |
| 14 | | | |
| 15 | | | |
| 16 | | | |
| 17 | | | |
| 18 | | | |
| 19 | | | |
| 20 | | | |
| 21 | | | |
| 22 | | | |
| 23 | | | |
| 24 | | | |

**EXERCISE 21-15**

| | A | B | C | D |
|---|---|---|---|---|
| 1 | Delaware Chemical Company | | | |
| 2 | Cost of Goods Sold Budget | | | |
| 3 | For the Month Ending June 30 | | | |
| 4 | | | | |
| 5 | | | | |
| 6 | | | | |
| 7 | | | | |
| 8 | | | | |
| 9 | | | | |
| 10 | | | | |
| 11 | | | | |
| 12 | | | | |
| 13 | | | | |
| 14 | | | | |
| 15 | | | | |
| 16 | | | | |
| 17 | | | | |
| 18 | | | | |
| 19 | | | | |
| 20 | | | | |
| 21 | | | | |
| 22 | | | | |
| 23 | | | | |
| 24 | | | | |
| 25 | | | | |
| 26 | | | | |
| 27 | | | | |
| 28 | | | | |
| 29 | | | | |
| 30 | | | | |
| 31 | | | | |
| 32 | | | | |
| 33 | | | | |
| 34 | | | | |
| 35 | | | | |
| 36 | | | | |

**EXERCISE  21-16**

| | A | B | C | D |
|---|---|---|---|---|
| 1 | MingWare Ceramics Inc. | | | |
| 2 | Cost of Goods Sold Budget | | | |
| 3 | For the Month Ending September 30 | | | |
| 4 | | | | |
| 5 | | | | |
| 6 | | | | |
| 7 | | | | |
| 8 | | | | |
| 9 | | | | |
| 10 | | | | |
| 11 | | | | |
| 12 | | | | |
| 13 | | | | |
| 14 | | | | |
| 15 | | | | |
| 16 | | | | |
| 17 | | | | |
| 18 | | | | |
| 19 | | | | |
| 20 | | | | |
| 21 | | | | |
| 22 | | | | |
| 23 | | | | |
| 24 | | | | |
| 25 | | | | |
| 26 | | | | |
| 27 | | | | |
| 28 | | | | |
| 29 | | | | |
| 30 | | | | |
| 31 | | | | |
| 32 | | | | |

**EXERCISE 21-17**

| | A | B | C | D |
|---|---|---|---|---|
| 1 | Pet Place Supplies Inc. | | | |
| 2 | Schedule of Cash Collections from Sales | | | |
| 3 | For the Three Months Ending July 31 | | | |
| 4 | | May | June | July |
| 5 | | | | |
| 6 | | | | |
| 7 | | | | |
| 8 | | | | |
| 9 | | | | |
| 10 | | | | |
| 11 | | | | |
| 12 | | | | |
| 13 | | | | |
| 14 | | | | |
| 15 | | | | |
| 16 | | | | |
| 17 | | | | |
| 18 | | | | |
| 19 | | | | |
| 20 | | | | |
| 21 | | | | |
| 22 | | | | |
| 23 | | | | |
| 24 | | | | |
| 25 | | | | |
| 26 | | | | |
| 27 | | | | |

**EXERCISE 21-18**

| | A | B | C | D |
|---|---|---|---|---|
| 1 | OfficeMart Inc. | | | |
| 2 | Schedule of Cash Collections from Sales | | | |
| 3 | For the Three Months Ending December 31 | | | |
| 4 | | October | November | December |
| 5 | | | | |
| 6 | | | | |
| 7 | | | | |
| 8 | | | | |
| 9 | | | | |
| 10 | | | | |
| 11 | | | | |
| 12 | | | | |
| 13 | | | | |
| 14 | | | | |
| 15 | | | | |
| 16 | | | | |
| 17 | | | | |
| 18 | | | | |
| 19 | | | | |
| 20 | | | | |
| 21 | | | | |
| 22 | | | | |
| 23 | | | | |
| 24 | | | | |
| 25 | | | | |
| 26 | | | | |
| 27 | | | | |
| 28 | | | | |
| 29 | | | | |
| 30 | | | | |
| 31 | | | | |
| 32 | | | | |

**EXERCISE 21-19**

| | A | B | C | D |
|---|---|---|---|---|
| 1 | Horizon Financial Inc. | | | |
| 2 | Schedule of Cash Payments for Selling and Administrative Expenses | | | |
| 3 | For the Three Months Ending May 31 | | | |
| 4 | | March | April | May |
| 5 | | | | |
| 6 | | | | |
| 7 | | | | |
| 8 | | | | |
| 9 | | | | |
| 10 | | | | |
| 11 | | | | |
| 12 | | | | |
| 13 | | | | |
| 14 | | | | |
| 15 | | | | |
| 16 | | | | |
| 17 | | | | |
| 18 | | | | |
| 19 | | | | |
| 20 | | | | |
| 21 | | | | |
| 22 | | | | |

**EXERCISE 21-20**

|   | A | B | C | D |
|---|---|---|---|---|
| 1 | Eastgate Physical Therapy Inc. | | | |
| 2 | Schedule of Cash Payments for Operations | | | |
| 3 | For the Three Months Ending March 31 | | | |
| 4 |   | January | February | March |
| 5 |   |   |   |   |
| 6 |   |   |   |   |
| 7 |   |   |   |   |
| 8 |   |   |   |   |
| 9 |   |   |   |   |
| 10 |   |   |   |   |
| 11 |   |   |   |   |
| 12 |   |   |   |   |
| 13 |   |   |   |   |
| 14 |   |   |   |   |
| 15 |   |   |   |   |
| 16 |   |   |   |   |
| 17 |   |   |   |   |
| 18 |   |   |   |   |
| 19 |   |   |   |   |
| 20 |   |   |   |   |
| 21 |   |   |   |   |
| 22 |   |   |   |   |
| 23 |   |   |   |   |
| 24 |   |   |   |   |

**EXERCISE 21-21**

|   | A | B | C | D | E |
|---|---|---|---|---|---|
| 1 | Omicron Inc. | | | | |
| 2 | Capital Expenditures Budget | | | | |
| 3 | For the Four Years Ending December 31, 20Y6–20Y9 | | | | |
| 4 |   | 20Y6 | 20Y7 | 20Y8 | 20Y9 |
| 5 |   |   |   |   |   |
| 6 |   |   |   |   |   |
| 7 |   |   |   |   |   |
| 8 |   |   |   |   |   |
| 9 |   |   |   |   |   |
| 10 |   |   |   |   |   |
| 11 |   |   |   |   |   |
| 12 |   |   |   |   |   |
| 13 |   |   |   |   |   |
| 14 |   |   |   |   |   |

**PROBLEM 21-1 ___**

1.

|  | UNIT SALES, YEAR ENDED 20Y8 | | INCREASE (DECREASE) ACTUAL OVER BUDGET | |
|---|---|---|---|---|
|  | BUDGET | ACTUAL SALES | AMOUNT | PERCENT |
|  |  |  |  |  |
|  |  |  |  |  |
|  |  |  |  |  |
|  |  |  |  |  |
|  |  |  |  |  |
|  |  |  |  |  |
|  |  |  |  |  |
|  |  |  |  |  |
|  |  |  |  |  |
|  |  |  |  |  |

2.

|  | 20Y8 ACTUAL UNITS | PERCENTAGE INCREASE (DECREASE) | 20Y9 BUDGETED UNITS (ROUNDED) |
|---|---|---|---|
|  |  |  |  |
|  |  |  |  |
|  |  |  |  |
|  |  |  |  |
|  |  |  |  |
|  |  |  |  |
|  |  |  |  |
|  |  |  |  |
|  |  |  |  |
|  |  |  |  |

**PROBLEM 21-1 ___, Concluded**

3.

| | A | B | C | D |
|---|---|---|---|---|
| 1 | | | | |
| 2 | | Sales Budget | | |
| 3 | | | | |
| 4 | Product and Area | Unit Sales Volume | Unit Selling Price | Total Sales |
| 5 | | | | |
| 6 | | | | |
| 7 | | | | |
| 8 | | | | |
| 9 | | | | |
| 10 | | | | |
| 11 | | | | |
| 12 | | | | |
| 13 | | | | |
| 14 | | | | |
| 15 | | | | |
| 16 | | | | |
| 17 | | | | |
| 18 | | | | |
| 19 | | | | |
| 20 | | | | |

**PROBLEM 21-2 ___**

1.

|  | A | B | C | D |
|---|---|---|---|---|
| 1 | | | | |
| 2 | Sales Budget | | | |
| 3 | | | | |
| 4 | Product and Area | Unit Sales Volume | Unit Selling Price | Total Sales |
| 5 | | | | |
| 6 | | | | |
| 7 | | | | |
| 8 | | | | |
| 9 | | | | |
| 10 | | | | |
| 11 | | | | |
| 12 | | | | |
| 13 | | | | |
| 14 | | | | |
| 15 | | | | |
| 16 | | | | |
| 17 | | | | |
| 18 | | | | |

2.

|  | A | B | C |
|---|---|---|---|
| 1 | | | |
| 2 | Production Budget | | |
| 3 | | | |
| 4 | | Units | |
| 5 | | | |
| 6 | | | |
| 7 | | | |
| 8 | | | |
| 9 | | | |
| 10 | | | |
| 11 | | | |
| 12 | | | |
| 13 | | | |
| 14 | | | |
| 15 | | | |
| 16 | | | |

**PROBLEM 21-2 ___ , Continued**

3.

| | A | B | C | D | E | F |
|---|---|---|---|---|---|---|
| 1 | | | | | | |
| 2 | | **Direct Materials Purchases Budget** | | | | |
| 3 | | | | | | |
| 4 | | | | | | |
| 5 | | | | | | |
| 6 | | | | | | |
| 7 | | | | | | |
| 8 | | | | | | |
| 9 | | | | | | |
| 10 | | | | | | |
| 11 | | | | | | |
| 12 | | | | | | |
| 13 | | | | | | |
| 14 | | | | | | |
| 15 | | | | | | |
| 16 | | | | | | |
| 17 | | | | | | |
| 18 | | | | | | |
| 19 | | | | | | |
| 20 | | | | | | |
| 21 | | | | | | |
| 22 | | | | | | |
| 23 | | | | | | |
| 24 | | | | | | |
| 25 | | | | | | |
| 26 | | | | | | |
| 27 | | | | | | |
| 28 | | | | | | |
| 29 | | | | | | |
| 30 | | | | | | |
| 31 | | | | | | |
| 32 | | | | | | |
| 33 | | | | | | |
| 34 | | | | | | |
| 35 | | | | | | |
| 36 | | | | | | |
| 37 | | | | | | |
| 38 | | | | | | |
| 39 | | | | | | |
| 40 | | | | | | |
| 41 | | | | | | |
| 42 | | | | | | |

**PROBLEM 21-2 ___ , Concluded**

4.

| | A | B | C | D | E |
|---|---|---|---|---|---|
| 1 | | | | | |
| 2 | | Direct Labor Cost Budget | | | |
| 3 | | | | | |
| 4 | | ____ Department | ____ Department | ____ Department | Total |
| 5 | | | | | |
| 6 | | | | | |
| 7 | | | | | |
| 8 | | | | | |
| 9 | | | | | |
| 10 | | | | | |
| 11 | | | | | |
| 12 | | | | | |
| 13 | | | | | |
| 14 | | | | | |
| 15 | | | | | |
| 16 | | | | | |
| 17 | | | | | |
| 18 | | | | | |
| 19 | | | | | |
| 20 | | | | | |
| 21 | | | | | |
| 22 | | | | | |
| 23 | | | | | |
| 24 | | | | | |
| 25 | | | | | |
| 26 | | | | | |
| 27 | | | | | |
| 28 | | | | | |
| 29 | | | | | |
| 30 | | | | | |
| 31 | | | | | |
| 32 | | | | | |

**This Page Not Used.**

**PROBLEM 21-3 ___**

1.

| | A | B | C | D |
|---|---|---|---|---|
| 1 | | | | |
| 2 | Sales Budget | | | |
| 3 | | | | |
| 4 | | Unit Sales Volume | Unit Selling Price | Total Sales |
| 5 | | | | |
| 6 | | | | |
| 7 | | | | |
| 8 | | | | |
| 9 | | | | |
| 10 | | | | |

2.

| | A | B | C |
|---|---|---|---|
| 1 | | | |
| 2 | Production Budget | | |
| 3 | | | |
| 4 | | Units | |
| 5 | | | |
| 6 | | | |
| 7 | | | |
| 8 | | | |
| 9 | | | |
| 10 | | | |
| 11 | | | |
| 12 | | | |
| 13 | | | |
| 14 | | | |
| 15 | | | |

**PROBLEM 21-3 ___, Continued**

3.

| | A | B | C | D |
|---|---|---|---|---|
| 1 | | | | |
| 2 | Direct Materials Purchases Budget | | | |
| 3 | | | | |
| 4 | | | | Total |
| 5 | | | | |
| 6 | | | | |
| 7 | | | | |
| 8 | | | | |
| 9 | | | | |
| 10 | | | | |
| 11 | | | | |
| 12 | | | | |
| 13 | | | | |
| 14 | | | | |
| 15 | | | | |
| 16 | | | | |
| 17 | | | | |
| 18 | | | | |
| 19 | | | | |
| 20 | | | | |
| 21 | | | | |
| 22 | | | | |
| 23 | | | | |
| 24 | | | | |
| 25 | | | | |
| 26 | | | | |

**PROBLEM 21-3 ___, Continued**

**4.**

|   | A | B | C | D |
|---|---|---|---|---|
| 1 | | | | |
| 2 | | Direct Labor Cost Budget | | |
| 3 | | | | |
| 4 | | ‾‾‾‾ Department | ‾‾‾‾ Department | Total |
| 5 | | | | |
| 6 | | | | |
| 7 | | | | |
| 8 | | | | |
| 9 | | | | |
| 10 | | | | |
| 11 | | | | |
| 12 | | | | |
| 13 | | | | |
| 14 | | | | |
| 15 | | | | |
| 16 | | | | |
| 17 | | | | |
| 18 | | | | |
| 19 | | | | |
| 20 | | | | |

**5.**

|   | A | B |
|---|---|---|
| 1 | | |
| 2 | Factory Overhead Cost Budget | |
| 3 | | |
| 4 | | |
| 5 | | |
| 6 | | |
| 7 | | |
| 8 | | |
| 9 | | |
| 10 | | |

**PROBLEM 21-3 ___, Continued**

6.

| | A | B | C | D |
|---|---|---|---|---|
| 1 | | | | |
| 2 | **Cost of Goods Sold Budget** | | | |
| 3 | | | | |
| 4 | | | | |
| 5 | | | | |
| 6 | | | | |
| 7 | | | | |
| 8 | | | | |
| 9 | | | | |
| 10 | | | | |
| 11 | | | | |
| 12 | | | | |
| 13 | | | | |
| 14 | | | | |
| 15 | | | | |
| 16 | | | | |
| 17 | | | | |
| 18 | | | | |
| 19 | | | | |
| 20 | | | | |
| 21 | | | | |
| 22 | | | | |
| 23 | | | | |
| 24 | | | | |
| 25 | | | | |
| 26 | | | | |
| 27 | | | | |
| 28 | | | | |
| 29 | | | | |
| 30 | | | | |
| 31 | | | | |
| 32 | | | | |
| 33 | | | | |
| 34 | | | | |

**PROBLEM  21-3 ___,  Continued**

Supporting calculations:

|  |  |  |
|---|---|---|
|  |  |  |
|  |  |  |
|  |  |  |
|  |  |  |
|  |  |  |
|  |  |  |
|  |  |  |
|  |  |  |
|  |  |  |
|  |  |  |
|  |  |  |
|  |  |  |
|  |  |  |
|  |  |  |
|  |  |  |
|  |  |  |
|  |  |  |
|  |  |  |
|  |  |  |

**PROBLEM 21-3 ___, Continued**

7.

| | A | B | C |
|---|---|---|---|
| 1 | | | |
| 2 | **Selling and Administrative Expenses Budget** | | |
| 3 | | | |
| 4 | | | |
| 5 | | | |
| 6 | | | |
| 7 | | | |
| 8 | | | |
| 9 | | | |
| 10 | | | |
| 11 | | | |
| 12 | | | |
| 13 | | | |
| 14 | | | |
| 15 | | | |
| 16 | | | |
| 17 | | | |
| 18 | | | |
| 19 | | | |
| 20 | | | |
| 21 | | | |
| 22 | | | |
| 23 | | | |
| 24 | | | |

**PROBLEM  21-3 ___,  Concluded**

8.

| | A | B | C |
|---|---|---|---|
| 1 | | | |
| 2 | **Budgeted Income Statement** | | |
| 3 | | | |
| 4 | | | |
| 5 | | | |
| 6 | | | |
| 7 | | | |
| 8 | | | |
| 9 | | | |
| 10 | | | |
| 11 | | | |
| 12 | | | |
| 13 | | | |
| 14 | | | |
| 15 | | | |
| 16 | | | |
| 17 | | | |
| 18 | | | |
| 19 | | | |
| 20 | | | |

**This Page Not Used.**

**PROBLEM 21-4 ___**

1.

| | A | B | C | D |
|---|---|---|---|---|
| 1 | | | | |
| 2 | Cash Budget | | | |
| 3 | | | | |
| 4 | | | | |
| 5 | | | | |
| 6 | | | | |
| 7 | | | | |
| 8 | | | | |
| 9 | | | | |
| 10 | | | | |
| 11 | | | | |
| 12 | | | | |
| 13 | | | | |
| 14 | | | | |
| 15 | | | | |
| 16 | | | | |
| 17 | | | | |
| 18 | | | | |
| 19 | | | | |
| 20 | | | | |
| 21 | | | | |
| 22 | | | | |
| 23 | | | | |
| 24 | | | | |
| 25 | | | | |
| 26 | | | | |
| 27 | | | | |
| 28 | | | | |
| 29 | | | | |
| 30 | | | | |
| 31 | | | | |
| 32 | | | | |

**PROBLEM 21-4 ___, Continued**

Computations:

| | | | |
|---|---|---|---|
| | | | |
| | | | |
| | | | |
| | | | |
| | | | |
| | | | |
| | | | |
| | | | |
| | | | |
| | | | |
| | | | |
| | | | |
| | | | |
| | | | |
| | | | |
| | | | |
| | | | |
| | | | |
| | | | |
| | | | |
| | | | |
| | | | |
| | | | |
| | | | |
| | | | |
| | | | |
| | | | |
| | | | |
| | | | |
| | | | |
| | | | |
| | | | |
| | | | |
| | | | |
| | | | |

**PROBLEM  21-4 ___,  Concluded**

2. _____

_____

_____

_____

_____

_____

_____

_____

_____

_____

284

**This Page Not Used.**

**PROBLEM 21-5 ___**

1.

|   | A | B | C | D |
|---|---|---|---|---|
| 1 | | | | |
| 2 | **Budgeted Income Statement** | | | |
| 3 | | | | |
| 4 | | | | |
| 5 | | | | |
| 6 | | | | |
| 7 | | | | |
| 8 | | | | |
| 9 | | | | |
| 10 | | | | |
| 11 | | | | |
| 12 | | | | |
| 13 | | | | |
| 14 | | | | |
| 15 | | | | |
| 16 | | | | |
| 17 | | | | |
| 18 | | | | |
| 19 | | | | |
| 20 | | | | |
| 21 | | | | |
| 22 | | | | |
| 23 | | | | |
| 24 | | | | |
| 25 | | | | |
| 26 | | | | |
| 27 | | | | |
| 28 | | | | |
| 29 | | | | |
| 30 | | | | |
| 31 | | | | |
| 32 | | | | |
| 33 | | | | |
| 34 | | | | |
| 35 | | | | |
| 36 | | | | |
| 37 | | | | |
| 38 | | | | |
| 39 | | | | |
| 40 | | | | |
| 41 | | | | |
| 42 | | | | |

**PROBLEM 21-5 ___, Continued**

2.

| | A | B | C | D |
|---|---|---|---|---|
| 1 | | | | |
| 2 | Budgeted Balance Sheet | | | |
| 3 | | | | |
| 4 | | | | |
| 5 | | | | |
| 6 | | | | |
| 7 | | | | |
| 8 | | | | |
| 9 | | | | |
| 10 | | | | |
| 11 | | | | |
| 12 | | | | |
| 13 | | | | |
| 14 | | | | |
| 15 | | | | |
| 16 | | | | |
| 17 | | | | |
| 18 | | | | |
| 19 | | | | |
| 20 | | | | |
| 21 | | | | |
| 22 | | | | |
| 23 | | | | |
| 24 | | | | |
| 25 | | | | |
| 26 | | | | |
| 27 | | | | |
| 28 | | | | |

**PROBLEM 21-5 ___, Concluded**

Supporting calculations:

| | | | |
|---|---|---|---|
| | | | |
| | | | |
| | | | |
| | | | |
| | | | |
| | | | |
| | | | |
| | | | |
| | | | |
| | | | |
| | | | |
| | | | |
| | | | |
| | | | |
| | | | |
| | | | |
| | | | |
| | | | |
| | | | |
| | | | |
| | | | |
| | | | |
| | | | |
| | | | |
| | | | |
| | | | |
| | | | |
| | | | |
| | | | |
| | | | |

288

This Page Not Used.

## EXERCISE 22-1

| Ingredient | Quantity | × | Price | Total |
|---|---|---|---|---|
|  |  | × |  |  |
|  |  | × |  |  |
|  |  | × |  |  |
|  |  |  |  |  |
|  |  |  |  |  |

_____

_____

_____

_____

_____

## EXERCISE 22-2

**A.**

|  |  |  |
|---|---|---|
|  |  |  |
|  |  |  |
|  |  |  |
|  |  |  |
|  |  |  |
|  |  |  |

**B.** _____

_____

_____

_____

_____

_____

_____

_____

_____

_____

**EXERCISE 22-3**

**A.**

| | A | B |
|---|---|---|
| 1 | Genie in a Bottle Company | |
| 2 | Manufacturing Cost Budget | |
| 3 | For the Month Ended July 31 | |
| 4 | | Standard Cost at Planned Volume (400,000 Bottles) |
| 5 | | |
| 6 | | |
| 7 | | |
| 8 | | |
| 9 | | |
| 10 | | |
| 11 | | |
| 12 | | |
| 13 | | |
| 14 | | |
| 15 | | |
| 16 | | |

**B.**

| | A | B | C | D |
|---|---|---|---|---|
| 1 | Genie in a Bottle Company | | | |
| 2 | Manufacturing Costs—Budget Performance Report | | | |
| 3 | For the Month Ended July 31 | | | |
| 4 | | Actual Costs | Standard Cost at Actual Volume (406,000 Bottles) | Cost Variance—(Favorable) Unfavorable |
| 5 | | | | |
| 6 | | | | |
| 7 | | | | |
| 8 | | | | |
| 9 | | | | |
| 10 | | | | |
| 11 | | | | |
| 12 | | | | |
| 13 | | | | |
| 14 | | | | |
| 15 | | | | |
| 16 | | | | |
| 17 | | | | |
| 18 | | | | |

**EXERCISE 22-3, Concluded**

**C.** _____

_____

_____

_____

_____

**EXERCISE 22-4**

**A.** Price variance: _____

_____

_____

_____

_____

_____

_____

_____

Quantity variance: _____

_____

_____

_____

_____

_____

_____

_____

Total direct materials cost variance: _____

_____

_____

_____

_____

_____

_____

_____

**EXERCISE 22-4, Concluded**

B. _____

_____

_____

_____

_____

_____

_____

_____

_____

_____

_____

_____

_____

_____

_____

_____

_____

_____

_____

_____

_____

_____

_____

_____

_____

**EXERCISE 22-5**

Price variance: _____

_____

_____

_____

_____

_____

_____

Quantity variance: _____

_____

_____

_____

_____

_____

_____

Total direct materials cost variance: _____

_____

_____

_____

_____

_____

_____

_____

**EXERCISE 22-6**

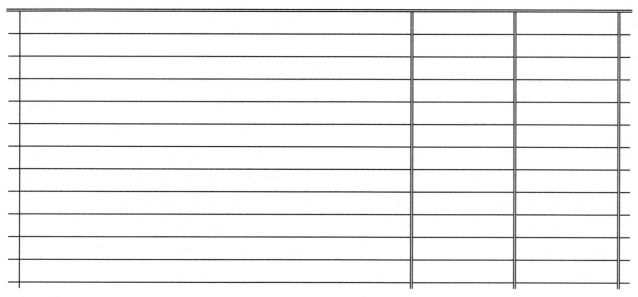

Alternate solution:

Proof:

_____

_____

_____

_____

_____

_____

_____

_____

_____

_____

**EXERCISE 22-7**

A.

| | | | |
|---|---|---|---|
| | | | |
| | | | |
| | | | |
| | | | |
| | | | |
| | | | |
| | | | |
| | | | |
| | | | |
| | | | |

B.

| | | | | | | |
|---|---|---|---|---|---|---|
| | | | | | | |
| | | | | | | |
| | | | | | | |
| | | | | | | |
| | | | | | | |
| | | | | | | |
| | | | | | | |
| | | | | | | |

## EXERCISE 22-8

**A.** Rate variance: _____

_____

_____

_____

_____

_____

_____

Time variance: _____

_____

_____

_____

_____

_____

_____

Total direct labor cost variance: _____

_____

_____

_____

_____

_____

_____

_____

**B.** _____

_____

_____

_____

_____

_____

_____

_____

_____

_____

**EXERCISE 22-9**

**A.** Rate variance: _____

_____

_____

_____

_____

_____

_____

Time variance: _____

_____

_____

_____

_____

_____

_____

Total direct labor cost variance: _____

_____

_____

_____

_____

_____

_____

**B.** Debit to Work in Process: _____

| | | |
|---|---|---|
| | | |
| | | |
| | | |
| | | |

**EXERCISE  22-10**

**A.  (1)** Cutting Department

Rate variance: _____

_____

_____

_____

_____

_____

_____

Time variance: _____

_____

_____

_____

_____

_____

_____

Total direct labor cost variance: _____

_____

_____

_____

_____

_____

_____

**EXERCISE 22-10, Continued**

(2) Sewing Department

Rate variance: _____

_____

_____

_____

_____

_____

_____

_____

Time variance: _____

_____

_____

_____

_____

_____

_____

_____

Total direct labor cost variance: _____

_____

_____

_____

_____

_____

_____

**EXERCISE 22-10, Concluded**

B. _____

_____

_____

_____

_____

_____

_____

_____

_____

_____

_____

_____

_____

**EXERCISE 22-11**

**A.** Rate variance: _____

_____

_____

_____

_____

_____

_____

Time variance: _____

_____

_____

_____

_____

_____

_____

Total direct labor cost variance: _____

_____

_____

_____

_____

_____

_____

**EXERCISE 22-11, Concluded**

**B.** _____

_____

_____

_____

_____

_____

_____

_____

_____

_____

_____

_____

_____

_____

_____

_____

**EXERCISE 22-12**

Step 1: _____

_____

_____

_____

_____

_____

_____

_____

_____

_____

_____

_____

_____

_____

_____

_____

_____

_____

_____

_____

Step 2: _____

_____

_____

| | | |
|---|---|---|
| | | |
| | | |
| | | |
| | | |
| | | |
| | | |
| | | |

**EXERCISE 22-12, Concluded**

Step 3: _____

_____

_____

| | | |
|---|---|---|
| | | |
| | | |
| | | |
| | | |
| | | |
| | | |
| | | |
| | | |
| | | |
| | | |
| | | |
| | | |
| | | |
| | | |
| | | |
| | | |
| | | |

**EXERCISE 22-13**

| | A | B | C | D |
|---|---|---|---|---|
| 1 | Leno Manufacturing Company | | | |
| 2 | Factory Overhead Cost Budget—Press Department | | | |
| 3 | For the Month Ended November 30 | | | |
| 4 | | | | |
| 5 | | | | |
| 6 | | | | |
| 7 | | | | |
| 8 | | | | |
| 9 | | | | |
| 10 | | | | |
| 11 | | | | |
| 12 | | | | |
| 13 | | | | |
| 14 | | | | |
| 15 | | | | |
| 16 | | | | |
| 17 | | | | |
| 18 | | | | |
| 19 | | | | |
| 20 | | | | |
| 21 | | | | |
| 22 | | | | |
| 23 | | | | |
| 24 | | | | |
| 25 | | | | |

**EXERCISE 22-14**

**A.**

| | A | B | C | D |
|---|---|---|---|---|
| 1 | Wiki Wiki Company | | | |
| 2 | Monthly Factory Overhead Cost Budget—Fabrication Department | | | |
| 3 | | | | |
| 4 | | | | |
| 5 | | | | |
| 6 | | | | |
| 7 | | | | |
| 8 | | | | |
| 9 | | | | |
| 10 | | | | |

**B.** Overhead applied to actual production:

Supporting calculations:

**EXERCISE 22-15**

Variable factory overhead controllable variance:

| | | |
|---|---|---|
| | | |
| | | |
| | | |
| | | |
| | | |
| | | |

Fixed factory overhead volume variance:

| | | |
|---|---|---|
| | | |
| | | |
| | | |
| | | |
| | | |
| | | |

Total factory overhead cost variance:

| | | |
|---|---|---|
| | | |
| | | |

**EXERCISE 22-15, Concluded**

Alternative Computation of Overhead Variances:

**EXERCISE 22-16**

**A.** Controllable variance:

| | | | |
|---|---|---|---|
| | | | |
| | | | |
| | | | |
| | | | |
| | | | |
| | | | |
| | | | |
| | | | |
| | | | |
| | | | |
| | | | |
| | | | |
| | | | |

**B.** Volume variance:

| | | |
|---|---|---|
| | | |
| | | |
| | | |
| | | |
| | | |
| | | |
| | | |
| | | |

Total factory overhead cost variance:

| | | | |
|---|---|---|---|
| | | | |
| | | | |
| | | | |
| | | | |

**EXERCISE 22-16, Concluded**

Alternative Computation of Overhead Variances:

**EXERCISE 22-17**

_____

_____

_____

_____

_____

_____

_____

_____

_____

Correct Determination of Factory Overhead Cost Variances:

| | | |
|---|---|---|
| | | |
| | | |
| | | |
| | | |
| | | |
| | | |
| | | |
| | | |
| | | |
| | | |
| | | |
| | | |
| | | |
| | | |
| | | |
| | | |
| | | |

## EXERCISE 22-17, Concluded

Alternative Computation of Overhead Variances:

**EXERCISE 22-18**

| | A | B | C | D | E |
|---|---|---|---|---|---|
| 1 | Tannin Products Inc. | | | | |
| 2 | Factory Overhead Cost Variance Report—Trim Department | | | | |
| 3 | For the Month Ended July 31 | | | | |
| 4 | Productive capacity for the month | | | | |
| 5 | Actual productive capacity used for the month | | | | |
| 6 | | | | | |
| 7 | | Budget (at actual production) | | Variances | |
| 8 | | | | | |
| 9 | | | Actual | Favorable | Unfavorable |
| 10 | | | | | |
| 11 | | | | | |
| 12 | | | | | |
| 13 | | | | | |
| 14 | | | | | |
| 15 | | | | | |
| 16 | | | | | |
| 17 | | | | | |
| 18 | | | | | |
| 19 | | | | | |
| 20 | | | | | |
| 21 | | | | | |
| 22 | | | | | |
| 23 | | | | | |
| 24 | | | | | |
| 25 | | | | | |
| 26 | | | | | |
| 27 | | | | | |
| 28 | | | | | |
| 29 | | | | | |
| 30 | | | | | |
| 31 | | | | | |
| 32 | | | | | |
| 33 | | | | | |
| 34 | | | | | |
| 35 | | | | | |
| 36 | | | | | |
| 37 | | | | | |
| 38 | | | | | |
| 39 | | | | | |
| 40 | | | | | |
| 41 | | | | | |
| 42 | | | | | |
| 43 | | | | | |
| 44 | | | | | |
| 45 | | | | | |
| 46 | | | | | |

**EXERCISE 22-18, Concluded**

Alternative Computation of Overhead Variances:

**EXERCISE 22-19**

**A. and B.**

**JOURNAL**                                                    PAGE

| | DATE | | DESCRIPTION | POST. REF. | DEBIT | CREDIT | |
|---|---|---|---|---|---|---|---|
| 1 | | | | | | | 1 |
| 2 | | | | | | | 2 |
| 3 | | | | | | | 3 |
| 4 | | | | | | | 4 |
| 5 | | | | | | | 5 |
| 6 | | | | | | | 6 |
| 7 | | | | | | | 7 |
| 8 | | | | | | | 8 |
| 9 | | | | | | | 9 |
| 10 | | | | | | | 10 |
| 11 | | | | | | | 11 |
| 12 | | | | | | | 12 |
| 13 | | | | | | | 13 |
| 14 | | | | | | | 14 |
| 15 | | | | | | | 15 |
| 16 | | | | | | | 16 |
| 17 | | | | | | | 17 |
| 18 | | | | | | | 18 |

**EXERCISE  22-20**

## JOURNAL

| | DATE | | DESCRIPTION | POST. REF. | DEBIT | CREDIT | |
|---|---|---|---|---|---|---|---|
| 1 | | | | | | | 1 |
| 2 | | | | | | | 2 |
| 3 | | | | | | | 3 |
| 4 | | | | | | | 4 |
| 5 | | | | | | | 5 |
| 6 | | | | | | | 6 |
| 7 | | | | | | | 7 |
| 8 | | | | | | | 8 |
| 9 | | | | | | | 9 |
| 10 | | | | | | | 10 |
| 11 | | | | | | | 11 |
| 12 | | | | | | | 12 |
| 13 | | | | | | | 13 |
| 14 | | | | | | | 14 |
| 15 | | | | | | | 15 |

**EXERCISE 22-21**

*Income Statement*

| | FAVORABLE | UNFAVORABLE | |
|---|---|---|---|
| | | | |
| | | | |
| | | | |
| | | | |
| | | | |
| | | | |
| | | | |
| | | | |
| | | | |
| | | | |
| | | | |
| | | | |
| | | | |
| | | | |
| | | | |
| | | | |
| | | | |
| | | | |
| | | | |
| | | | |
| | | | |
| | | | |
| | | | |
| | | | |

**EXERCISE 22-22**

**A. and B.**

| | Input Measure | Output Measure | Explanation |
|---|---|---|---|
| Average computer response time to customer "clicks" | | | |
| Dollar amount of returned goods | | | |
| Elapsed time between customer order and product delivery | | | |
| Maintenance dollars divided by hardware investment | | | |
| Number of customer complaints divided by the number of orders | | | |
| Number of misfilled orders divided by the number of orders | | | |
| Number of orders per warehouse employee | | | |
| Number of page faults or errors due to software programming errors | | | |
| Number of software fixes per week | | | |
| Server (computer) downtime | | | |
| Training dollars per programmer | | | |

**EXERCISE 22-23**

**A.** Input Measures: _____

_____

_____

_____

_____

_____

_____

_____

_____

Output Measures: _____

_____

_____

_____

_____

_____

_____

_____

_____

_____

_____

_____

**B.** _____

_____

_____

_____

_____

_____

_____

_____

_____

_____

_____

_____

**This Page Not Used.**

**PROBLEM 22-1 ___**

**A.**

| | | |
|---|---|---|
| | | |
| | | |
| | | |
| | | |
| | | |
| | | |

**B. Direct Materials Cost Variance**

Price variance: _____

_____

_____

_____

_____

_____

_____

Quantity variance: _____

_____

_____

_____

_____

_____

_____

Total direct materials cost variance: _____

_____

_____

_____

_____

_____

_____

**PROBLEM  22-1 ___ ,  Concluded**

## C.  Direct Labor Cost Variance

Rate variance: _____

_____

_____

_____

_____

_____

_____

Time variance: _____

_____

_____

_____

_____

_____

_____

Total direct labor cost variance: _____

_____

_____

_____

_____

_____

_____

**PROBLEM 22-2 ___**

1.  A.

|  |  |  | TOTAL |
|---|---|---|---|
|  |  |  |  |
|  |  |  |  |
|  |  |  |  |
|  |  |  |  |
|  |  |  |  |
|  |  |  |  |
|  |  |  |  |
|  |  |  |  |
|  |  |  |  |
|  |  |  |  |
|  |  |  |  |
|  |  |  |  |
|  |  |  |  |
|  |  |  |  |
|  |  |  |  |
|  |  |  |  |
|  |  |  |  |
|  |  |  |  |
|  |  |  |  |
|  |  |  |  |
|  |  |  |  |
|  |  |  |  |
|  |  |  |  |
|  |  |  |  |
|  |  |  |  |
|  |  |  |  |
|  |  |  |  |
|  |  |  |  |
|  |  |  |  |
|  |  |  |  |
|  |  |  |  |
|  |  |  |  |
|  |  |  |  |
|  |  |  |  |

**PROBLEM 22-2 ___, Continued**

B.

| | | | TOTAL |
|---|---|---|---|
| | | | |
| | | | |
| | | | |
| | | | |
| | | | |
| | | | |
| | | | |
| | | | |
| | | | |
| | | | |
| | | | |
| | | | |
| | | | |
| | | | |
| | | | |
| | | | |
| | | | |
| | | | |
| | | | |
| | | | |
| | | | |
| | | | |
| | | | |
| | | | |
| | | | |
| | | | |
| | | | |
| | | | |
| | | | |
| | | | |
| | | | |
| | | | |
| | | | |
| | | | |

**PROBLEM  22-2 \_\_\_,  Concluded**

2.  _____

    _____

    _____

    _____

    _____

    _____

    _____

    _____

    _____

    _____

    _____

    _____

This Page Not Used.

**PROBLEM 22-3 ___**

A. <u>**Direct Materials Cost Variance**</u>

Price variance: _____

_____

_____

_____

_____

_____

_____

Quantity variance: _____

_____

_____

_____

_____

_____

_____

Total direct materials cost variance: _____

_____

_____

_____

_____

_____

_____

**PROBLEM 22-3 ___, Continued**

**B. Direct Labor Cost Variance**

Rate variance: _____

_____

_____

_____

_____

_____

_____

Time variance: _____

_____

_____

_____

_____

_____

_____

_____

Total direct labor cost variance: _____

_____

_____

_____

_____

_____

_____

**PROBLEM  22-3 ___,  Continued**

## C. Factory Overhead Cost Variance

| | | |
|---|---|---|
| | | |
| | | |
| | | |
| | | |
| | | |
| | | |
| | | |
| | | |
| | | |
| | | |
| | | |
| | | |
| | | |
| | | |
| | | |
| | | |
| | | |
| | | |
| | | |
| | | |
| | | |
| | | |
| | | |
| | | |

**PROBLEM  22-3 ___,  Concluded**

Alternative Computation of Overhead Variances:

**PROBLEM 22-4 ___**

|   | A | B | C | D | E |
|---|---|---|---|---|---|
| 1 | | | | | |
| 2 | Factory Overhead Cost Variance Report—_____ Department | | | | |
| 3 | | | | | |
| 4 | Normal capacity for the month | | | | |
| 5 | Actual production for the month | | | | |
| 6 | | | | | |
| 7 | | | | Variances | |
| 8 | | Budget | Actual | Favorable | Unfavorable |
| 9 | | | | | |
| 10 | | | | | |
| 11 | | | | | |
| 12 | | | | | |
| 13 | | | | | |
| 14 | | | | | |
| 15 | | | | | |
| 16 | | | | | |
| 17 | | | | | |
| 18 | | | | | |
| 19 | | | | | |
| 20 | | | | | |
| 21 | | | | | |
| 22 | | | | | |
| 23 | | | | | |
| 24 | | | | | |
| 25 | | | | | |
| 26 | | | | | |
| 27 | | | | | |
| 28 | | | | | |
| 29 | | | | | |
| 30 | | | | | |
| 31 | | | | | |
| 32 | | | | | |
| 33 | | | | | |
| 34 | | | | | |
| 35 | | | | | |
| 36 | | | | | |
| 37 | | | | | |
| 38 | | | | | |
| 39 | | | | | |
| 40 | | | | | |
| 41 | | | | | |
| 42 | | | | | |
| 43 | | | | | |
| 44 | | | | | |
| 45 | | | | | |
| 46 | | | | | |

**PROBLEM  22-4 ___,  Concluded**

Alternative Computation of Overhead Variances:

**PROBLEM 22-5 ___**

1.

| | | |
|---|---|---|
| | | |
| | | |
| | | |
| | | |
| | | |
| | | |

_____

_____

_____

2.

| | | |
|---|---|---|
| | | |
| | | |
| | | |
| | | |
| | | |

_____

_____

_____

**PROBLEM 22-5 ___, Continued**

**3.**

| | | |
|---|---|---|
| | | |
| | | |
| | | |
| | | |
| | | |
| | | |

**4.**

| | | |
|---|---|---|
| | | |
| | | |
| | | |
| | | |
| | | |
| | | |

**PROBLEM 22-5 ___, Concluded**

5.

| | | |
|---|---|---|
| | | |
| | | |
| | | |
| | | |
| | | |
| | | |
| | | |

6.

This Page Not Used.

**COMPREHENSIVE PROBLEM 5**

**Part A**

1. _____
_____
_____
_____
_____
_____
_____
_____
_____
_____
_____
_____

2.

|  |  |  |
|---|---|---|
|  |  |  |
|  |  |  |
|  |  |  |
|  |  |  |
|  |  |  |
|  |  |  |
|  |  |  |

3.

|  |  |
|---|---|
|  |  |
|  |  |
|  |  |
|  |  |
|  |  |

4. _____
_____
_____
_____

**COMPREHENSIVE PROBLEM 5, Continued**

**Part B**

**5.**

| | CASES |
|---|---|
| *Production Budget* | |
| | |
| | |
| | |
| | |
| | |

**6.**

*Direct Materials Purchases Budget*

| | CREAM BASE (OZS.) | NATURAL OILS (OZS.) | BOTTLES (BOTTLES) | TOTAL |
|---|---|---|---|---|
| | | | | |
| | | | | |
| | | | | |
| | | | | |
| | | | | |
| | | | | |
| | | | | |
| | | | | |
| | | | | |
| | | | | |
| | | | | |
| | | | | |
| | | | | |
| | | | | |
| | | | | |
| | | | | |

**COMPREHENSIVE PROBLEM 5, Continued**

**7.**

| | Direct Labor Budget | | | | |
|---|---|---|---|---|---|
| | | MIXING | FILLING | TOTAL | |
| | | | | | |
| | | | | | |
| | | | | | |
| | | | | | |
| | | | | | |
| | | | | | |
| | | | | | |
| | | | | | |

**8.**

| | Factory Overhead Budget | | | | |
|---|---|---|---|---|---|
| | | | | | |
| | | | | | |
| | | | | | |
| | | | | | |
| | | | | | |
| | | | | | |
| | | | | | |
| | | | | | |

**COMPREHENSIVE PROBLEM 5, Continued**

9.

| Budgeted Income Statement | | | |
|---|---|---|---|
|  |  |  |  |
|  |  |  |  |
|  |  |  |  |
|  |  |  |  |
|  |  |  |  |
|  |  |  |  |
|  |  |  |  |
|  |  |  |  |
|  |  |  |  |
|  |  |  |  |
|  |  |  |  |
|  |  |  |  |
|  |  |  |  |
|  |  |  |  |
|  |  |  |  |
|  |  |  |  |
|  |  |  |  |
|  |  |  |  |
|  |  |  |  |
|  |  |  |  |
|  |  |  |  |
|  |  |  |  |
|  |  |  |  |
|  |  |  |  |
|  |  |  |  |
|  |  |  |  |
|  |  |  |  |
|  |  |  |  |
|  |  |  |  |
|  |  |  |  |

## COMPREHENSIVE PROBLEM 5, Continued

## Part C

**10.** Direct Materials Price Variance:

|  | CREAM BASE | NATURAL OILS | BOTTLES |  |
|---|---|---|---|---|
|  |  |  |  |  |
|  |  |  |  |  |
|  |  |  |  |  |
|  |  |  |  |  |
|  |  |  |  |  |
|  |  |  |  |  |
|  |  |  |  |  |
|  |  |  |  |  |
|  |  |  |  |  |
|  |  |  |  |  |
|  |  |  |  |  |
|  |  |  |  |  |
|  |  |  |  |  |
|  |  |  |  |  |
|  |  |  |  |  |
|  |  |  |  |  |

## COMPREHENSIVE PROBLEM 5, Continued

Direct Materials Quantity Variance:

| | CREAM BASE | NATURAL OILS | BOTTLES |
|---|---|---|---|
| | | | |
| | | | |
| | | | |
| | | | |
| | | | |
| | | | |
| | | | |
| | | | |
| | | | |
| | | | |
| | | | |
| | | | |
| | | | |
| | | | |
| | | | |
| | | | |
| | | | |
| | | | |
| | | | |
| | | | |
| | | | |
| | | | |
| | | | |
| | | | |

_____

_____

_____

_____

_____

_____

_____

_____

_____

**COMPREHENSIVE PROBLEM 5, Continued**

**11.** Direct Labor Rate Variance:

| | MIXING DEPARTMENT | FILLING DEPARTMENT | |
|---|---|---|---|
| | | | |
| | | | |
| | | | |
| | | | |
| | | | |
| | | | |

_____

_____

_____

_____

_____

_____

_____

**COMPREHENSIVE PROBLEM 5, Continued**

Direct Labor Time Variance:

| | MIXING DEPARTMENT | FILLING DEPARTMENT |
|---|---|---|
| | | |
| | | |
| | | |
| | | |
| | | |
| | | |
| | | |
| | | |
| | | |
| | | |
| | | |
| | | |
| | | |
| | | |
| | | |
| | | |
| | | |
| | | |
| | | |

## COMPREHENSIVE PROBLEM 5, Continued

**12.** Factory Overhead Controllable Variance:

| | | |
|---|---|---|
| | | |
| | | |
| | | |
| | | |
| | | |
| | | |
| | | |

**13.** Factory Overhead Volume Variance:

| | | |
|---|---|---|
| | | |
| | | |
| | | |
| | | |
| | | |
| | | |
| | | |

**COMPREHENSIVE PROBLEM 5, Continued**

Alternative Computation of Overhead Variances:

**COMPREHENSIVE PROBLEM 5, Concluded**

14. _____

_____

_____

_____

_____

_____

_____

_____

_____

_____

_____

_____

This Page Not Used.

## EXERCISE 23-1

**A.**

### Garland Company
### Budget Performance Report—Vice President, Production
### For the Month Ended November 30

| Plant | Budget | Actual | Over Budget | Under Budget |
|---|---|---|---|---|
| Eastern Region | $2,300,000 | $2,287,900 | | $(12,100) |
| Central Region | 3,000,000 | 2,988,400 | | (11,600) |
| Western Region | (G) _____ | (H) _____ | (I) $ _____ | _____ |
| | (J) $ _____ | (K) $ _____ | (L) $ _____ | $(23,700) |

### Garland Company
### Budget Performance Report—Manager, Western Region Plant
### For the Month Ended November 30

| Department | Budget | Actual | Over Budget | Under Budget |
|---|---|---|---|---|
| Chip Fabrication | (A) $ _____ | (B) $ _____ | (C) $ _____ | |
| Electronic Assembly | 700,000 | 703,200 | 3,200 | |
| Final Assembly | 525,000 | 516,600 | _____ | $(8,400) |
| | (D) $ _____ | (E) $ _____ | (F) $ _____ | $(8,400) |

### Garland Company
### Budget Performance Report—Supervisor, Chip Fabrication
### For the Month Ended November 30

| Cost | Budget | Actual | Over Budget | Under Budget |
|---|---|---|---|---|
| Factory wages | $ 82,000 | $ 95,500 | $13,500 | |
| Materials | 120,000 | 115,300 | | $(4,700) |
| Power and light | 45,000 | 49,950 | 4,950 | |
| Maintenance | 28,000 | 37,200 | 9,200 | |
| | $275,000 | $297,950 | $27,650 | $(4,700) |

**EXERCISE 23-1, Concluded**

B. _____

_____

_____

_____

_____

_____

_____

_____

_____

_____

_____

_____

_____

_____

_____

_____

_____

_____

_____

_____

_____

_____

**EXERCISE 23-2**

*Divisional Income Statements*

| | COMMERCIAL DIVISION | RESIDENTIAL DIVISION |
|---|---|---|
| | | |
| | | |
| | | |
| | | |
| | | |
| | | |
| | | |
| | | |
| | | |
| | | |

**EXERCISE 23-3**

**A.** Legal: _____

_____

**B.** Duplication services: _____

_____

**C.** Electronic data processing: _____

_____

**D.** Central purchasing: _____

_____

**E.** Telecommunications: _____

_____

**F.** Accounts receivable: _____

_____

**EXERCISE 23-4**

**A.** Accounts Receivable: _____

**B.** Central Purchasing: _____

**C.** Computer Support: _____

**D.** Conferences: _____

**E.** Employee Travel: _____

**F.** Payroll Accounting: _____

**G.** Telecommunications: _____

**H.** Training: _____

**EXERCISE 23-5**

**A.**

| | RESIDENTIAL | COMMERCIAL | GOVERNMENT CONTRACT | TOTAL | |
|---|---|---|---|---|---|
| | | | | | |
| | | | | | |
| | | | | | |
| | | | | | |
| | | | | | |
| | | | | | |
| | | | | | |
| | | | | | |
| | | | | | |
| | | | | | |
| | | | | | |

**EXERCISE 23-5, Continued**

**B.**

| | | | |
|---|---|---|---|
| | | | |
| | | | |
| | | | |
| | | | |
| | | | |
| | | | |
| | | | |

| | RESIDENTIAL | COMMERCIAL | GOVERNMENT CONTRACT | TOTAL |
|---|---|---|---|---|
| | | | | |
| | | | | |
| | | | | |
| | | | | |
| | | | | |
| | | | | |
| | | | | |
| | | | | |
| | | | | |
| | | | | |
| | | | | |
| | | | | |
| | | | | |
| | | | | |
| | | | | |
| | | | | |
| | | | | |

**EXERCISE 23-5, Concluded**

C. _____

_____

_____

_____

_____

_____

_____

_____

_____

_____

_____

_____

_____

_____

_____

**EXERCISE 23-6**

**A.** Help desk: _____

_____

_____

Network center: _____

_____

_____

Electronic mail: _____

_____

_____

Smartphone support: _____

_____

_____

**B.** Help desk charge: _____

_____

_____

Network center charge: _____

_____

_____

Electronic mail charge: _____

_____

_____

Smartphone support charge: _____

_____

_____

**EXERCISE 23-7**

*Divisional Income Statements*

| | CONSUMER DIVISION | COMMERCIAL DIVISION |
|---|---|---|
| | | |
| | | |
| | | |
| | | |
| | | |
| | | |
| | | |
| | | |
| | | |
| | | |
| | | |
| | | |
| | | |
| | | |

Supporting calculations:

_____
_____
_____
_____
_____
_____
_____
_____
_____
_____
_____
_____

**EXERCISE 23-8**

A. _____

_____

_____

_____

_____

_____

_____

_____

_____

_____

_____

_____

_____

_____

**EXERCISE 23-8, Concluded**

**B.**

---

*Divisional Income Statements*

| | PASSENGER DIVISION | CARGO DIVISION |
|---|---|---|
| | | |
| | | |
| | | |
| | | |
| | | |
| | | |
| | | |
| | | |
| | | |
| | | |
| | | |
| | | |
| | | |

Supporting calculations:

_____

_____

_____

_____

_____

_____

_____

_____

_____

_____

_____

_____

_____

_____

_____

**EXERCISE 23-9**

*Divisional Income Statements*

| | WINTER SPORTS DIVISION | SUMMER SPORTS DIVISION |
|---|---|---|
| | | |
| | | |
| | | |
| | | |
| | | |
| | | |
| | | |
| | | |
| | | |
| | | |
| | | |
| | | |
| | | |
| | | |
| | | |
| | | |
| | | |
| | | |
| | | |
| | | |
| | | |
| | | |
| | | |

## EXERCISE 23-9, Concluded

Supporting calculations:

_____

_____

_____

_____

_____

_____

_____

_____

_____

_____

_____

_____

| | | | |
|---|---|---|---|
| | | | |
| | | | |
| | | | |
| | | | |
| | | | |
| | | | |
| | | | |
| | | | |
| | | | |
| | | | |
| | | | |
| | | | |
| | | | |
| | | | |
| | | | |
| | | | |
| | | | |
| | | | |

**EXERCISE  23-10**

**A.** Retail Division: _____

Commercial Division: _____

Internet Division: _____

**B.** _____

**EXERCISE  23-11**

**A.**

| | RETAIL DIVISION | COMMERCIAL DIVISION | INTERNET DIVISION | |
|---|---|---|---|---|
| | | | | |
| | | | | |
| | | | | |
| | | | | |
| | | | | |
| | | | | |
| | | | | |
| | | | | |
| | | | | |

**B.** _____

**EXERCISE  23-12**

| Return on Investment | = | Profit Margin | × | Investment Turnover |
|---|---|---|---|---|
| 13.2% | = | 6% | × | **(A)** _____ |
| **(B)** _____ | = | 10% | × | 1.80 |
| 10.5% | = | **(C)** _____ | × | 1.50 |
| 15% | = | 5% | × | **(D)** _____ |
| **(E)** _____ | = | 12% | × | 1.10 |

**EXERCISE 23-13**

**A.** _____

_____

_____

_____

_____

_____

_____

_____

_____

_____

_____

**B.** _____

_____

_____

_____

_____

_____

_____

_____

_____

_____

_____

_____

_____

_____

_____

_____

_____

_____

_____

**EXERCISE 23-14**

A. _____

_____

_____

Media Networks: _____

_____

_____

_____

_____

_____

_____

Parks and Resorts: _____

_____

_____

_____

_____

_____

_____

Studio Entertainment: _____

_____

_____

_____

_____

_____

_____

Consumer Products: _____

_____

_____

_____

_____

_____

_____

**EXERCISE 23-14, Concluded**

**B.** _____

_____

_____

_____

_____

_____

_____

_____

_____

_____

_____

_____

_____

_____

## EXERCISE 23-15

| Invested Assets | Income from Operations | Return on Investment | Minimum Return on Investment | Minimum Acceptable Income from Operations | Residual Income |
|---|---|---|---|---|---|
| $925,000 | $185,000 | (A)_____ | 15% | (B) $_____ | (C) $_____ |
| $775,000 | (D) $_____ | (E)_____ | (F) _____ | $93,000 | $23,250 |
| $450,000 | (G) $_____ | 18% | (H) _____ | $58,500 | (I) $_____ |
| $610,000 | $97,600 | (J) _____ | 12% | (K) $_____ | (L) $_____ |

Calculations:

(A) _____

(B) _____

(C) _____

(D) _____

(E) _____

(F) _____

(G) _____

(H) _____

(I) _____

(J) _____

(K) _____

(L) _____

**EXERCISE 23-16**

**A.**

|  | Sales | Income from Operations | Invested Assets | Return on Investment | Profit Margin | Investment Turnover |
|---|---|---|---|---|---|---|
| North | $860,000 | (A) $ _____ | (B) $ _____ | 17.5% | 7.0% | (C) _____ |
| South | (D) $ _____ | $51,300 | (E) $ _____ | (F) _____ | 4.5% | 3.8 |
| East | $1,020,000 | (G) $ _____ | $680,000 | 15.0% | (H) _____ | (I) _____ |
| West | $1,120,000 | $89,600 | $560,000 | (J) _____ | (K) _____ | (L) _____ |

Calculations:

(A) _____

(B) _____

(C) _____

(D) _____

(E) _____

(F) _____

(G) _____

(H) _____

(I) _____

(J) _____

(K) _____

(L) _____

**B.** North Division: _____

_____

South Division: _____

_____

East Division: _____

_____

West Division: _____

_____

**C. (1)** _____

**(2)** _____

## EXERCISE 23-17

Average card member spending: _____

_____

Cards in force: _____

_____

Earnings growth: _____

_____

Hours of credit consultant training: _____

_____

Investment in information technology: _____

_____

Number of card choices: _____

_____

Number of Internet features: _____

_____

Number of merchant signings: _____

_____

Number of new card launches: _____

_____

Return on equity: _____

_____

Revenue growth: _____

_____

**EXERCISE 23-18**

**EXERCISE 23-19**

**A.** _____

_____

_____

_____

_____

_____

_____

_____

**B.** _____

_____

_____

_____

_____

_____

_____

_____

**C.** _____

_____

_____

_____

_____

_____

_____

_____

**EXERCISE  23-20**

A. _____

_____

_____

_____

_____

_____

_____

_____

_____

_____

B. _____

_____

_____

_____

_____

_____

_____

_____

_____

_____

_____

**EXERCISE 23-20, Concluded**

C. _____

_____

_____

_____

_____

_____

_____

_____

_____

_____

_____

D. _____

_____

_____

_____

_____

_____

_____

_____

_____

_____

_____

_____

_____

_____

_____

_____

_____

_____

_____

_____

**PROBLEM 23-1 ___**

**1.**

| | | BUDGET | ACTUAL | OVER BUDGET | UNDER BUDGET |
|---|---|---|---|---|---|
| *Budget Performance Report — _____* | | | | | |
| | | | | | |
| | | | | | |
| | | | | | |
| | | | | | |
| | | | | | |
| | | | | | |
| | | | | | |
| | | | | | |
| | | | | | |
| | | | | | |
| | | | | | |
| | | | | | |
| | | | | | |
| | | | | | |

**2.** _____

_____

_____

_____

_____

_____

_____

_____

_____

_____

_____

_____

_____

_____

_____

**This Page Not Used.**

**PROBLEM  23-2 ___**

1.

*Divisional Income Statements*

| | | | |
|---|---|---|---|
| | | | |
| | | | |
| | | | |
| | | | |
| | | | |
| | | | |
| | | | |
| | | | |
| | | | |
| | | | |
| | | | |
| | | | |

Supporting calculations:

| | | | | |
|---|---|---|---|---|
| | | | | |
| | | | | |
| | | | | |

**PROBLEM 23-2 ___, Concluded**

2. _____

_____

_____

_____

_____

_____

_____

_____

_____

_____

_____

3. _____

_____

_____

_____

_____

_____

_____

_____

_____

_____

_____

_____

_____

_____

_____

_____

_____

_____

_____

_____

_____

**PROBLEM  23-3 ___**

1.

| | | *Divisional Income Statements* | | |
|---|---|---|---|---|
| | | | | |
| | | | | |
| | | | | |
| | | | | |
| | | | | |
| | | | | |
| | | | | |
| | | | | |
| | | | | |

**PROBLEM 23-3 ___, Continued**

2. _____

_____

_____

_____

_____

_____

_____

_____

_____

_____

_____

_____

_____

_____

_____

_____

_____

_____

_____

_____

_____

_____

_____

_____

_____

_____

_____

_____

_____

_____

_____

_____

_____

**PROBLEM 23-3 ___, Concluded**

3. _____

_____

_____

_____

_____

_____

_____

_____

_____

_____

_____

_____

_____

_____

_____

**This Page Not Used.**

**PROBLEM 23-4 ___**

1. _____

_____

_____

_____

_____

_____

_____

_____

_____

_____

_____

_____

_____

_____

_____

_____

**PROBLEM 23-4 ___, Continued**

2.

*Estimated Income Statements*

|  | PROPOSAL 1 | PROPOSAL 2 | PROPOSAL 3 |
|---|---|---|---|
|  |  |  |  |
|  |  |  |  |
|  |  |  |  |
|  |  |  |  |
|  |  |  |  |
|  |  |  |  |
|  |  |  |  |
|  |  |  |  |
|  |  |  |  |
|  |  |  |  |
|  |  |  |  |
|  |  |  |  |
|  |  |  |  |
|  |  |  |  |
|  |  |  |  |
|  |  |  |  |

**PROBLEM 23-4 ___, Continued**

3. _____

_____

_____

_____

_____

_____

_____

_____

_____

_____

_____

_____

_____

_____

_____

_____

_____

_____

_____

_____

_____

_____

_____

_____

_____

4. _____

_____

_____

**PROBLEM 23-4 ___, Concluded**

5. _____

_____

_____

_____

_____

_____

_____

_____

_____

_____

_____

_____

_____

_____

_____

_____

_____

_____

**PROBLEM  23-5 ___**

1.

|  | | | |
|---|---|---|---|
| *Divisional Income Statements* | | | |
|  | | | |
|  | | | |
|  | | | |
|  | | | |
|  | | | |
|  | | | |
|  | | | |
|  | | | |
|  | | | |

**PROBLEM 23-5 ___, Continued**

2. _____

_____

_____

_____

_____

_____

_____

_____

_____

_____

_____

_____

_____

_____

_____

_____

_____

_____

_____

_____

_____

_____

_____

_____

_____

_____

3. _____

_____

_____

_____

_____

**PROBLEM 23-5 ___, Concluded**

4. _____

———————————————————————————————————————

———————————————————————————————————————

———————————————————————————————————————

———————————————————————————————————————

———————————————————————————————————————

———————————————————————————————————————

———————————————————————————————————————

———————————————————————————————————————

———————————————————————————————————————

———————————————————————————————————————

———————————————————————————————————————

———————————————————————————————————————

———————————————————————————————————————

———————————————————————————————————————

———————————————————————————————————————

———————————————————————————————————————

———————————————————————————————————————

———————————————————————————————————————

———————————————————————————————————————

———————————————————————————————————————

———————————————————————————————————————

———————————————————————————————————————

———————————————————————————————————————

———————————————————————————————————————

———————————————————————————————————————

———————————————————————————————————————

**This Page Not Used.**

**PROBLEM  23-6 ___**

1.  _____

    _____

    _____

    _____

    _____

**PROBLEM 23-6 ___, Continued**

2. _____

_____

_____

_____

_____

_____

_____

_____

_____

_____

_____

_____

_____

_____

_____

_____

_____

_____

_____

_____

_____

_____

_____

_____

_____

_____

_____

_____

_____

_____

_____

_____

_____

_____

_____

_____

**PROBLEM 23-6 ___, Continued**

3.

| | | | | | | | |
|---|---|---|---|---|---|---|---|
| | | | | | | | |

| | | | | TOTAL |
|---|---|---|---|---|---|
| | | | | |
| | | | | |
| | | | | |
| | | | | |
| | | | | |
| | | | | |
| | | | | |
| | | | | |
| | | | | |
| | | | | |
| | | | | |
| | | | | |
| | | | | |
| | | | | |
| | | | | |
| | | | | |
| | | | | |
| | | | | |
| | | | | |
| | | | | |
| | | | | |
| | | | | |
| | | | | |
| | | | | |
| | | | | |
| | | | | |

*Divisional Income Statements*

**PROBLEM 23-6 ___, Continued**

4. _____

_____

_____

_____

_____

_____

_____

_____

_____

_____

_____

_____

_____

_____

_____

_____

_____

_____

_____

_____

_____

_____

_____

_____

_____

_____

_____

_____

_____

_____

_____

_____

_____

**PROBLEM 23-6 ___, Concluded**

5. A. _____

_____

_____

_____

_____

_____

_____

_____

_____

B. _____

_____

_____

_____

_____

_____

_____

_____

_____

_____

**This Page Not Used.**

**EXERCISE 24-1**

**A.**

---

*Lease Machinery (Alternative 1) or Sell Machinery (Alternative 2)*

| | LEASE MACHINERY (ALTERNATIVE 1) | SELL MACHINERY (ALTERNATIVE 2) | DIFFERENTIAL EFFECT ON INCOME (ALTERNATIVE 2) |
|---|---|---|---|
| | | | |
| | | | |
| | | | |
| | | | |

**B.** _____

**EXERCISE 24-2**

---

*Lease Equipment (Alternative 1) or Buy Equipment (Alternative 2)*

| | LEASE EQUIPMENT (ALTERNATIVE 1) | BUY EQUIPMENT (ALTERNATIVE 2) | DIFFERENTIAL EFFECT ON INCOME (ALTERNATIVE 2) |
|---|---|---|---|
| | | | |
| | | | |
| | | | |
| | | | |
| | | | |
| | | | |
| | | | |
| | | | |
| | | | |

**EXERCISE 24-3**

**A.**

| | CONTINUE FRUIT COLA (ALTERNATIVE 1) | DISCONTINUE FRUIT COLA (ALTERNATIVE 2) | DIFFERENTIAL EFFECT ON INCOME (ALTERNATIVE 2) |
|---|---|---|---|
| *Continue Fruit Cola (Alternative 1) or Discontinue Fruit Cola (Alternative 2)* | | | |
| | | | |
| | | | |
| | | | |
| | | | |
| | | | |
| | | | |
| | | | |
| | | | |
| | | | |
| | | | |
| | | | |
| | | | |

**B.** _____

_____

_____

_____

**EXERCISE 24-4**

**A.**

| | CONTINUE CUPS (ALTERNATIVE 1) | DISCONTINUE CUPS (ALTERNATIVE 2) | DIFFERENTIAL EFFECT ON INCOME (ALTERNATIVE 2) | |
|---|---|---|---|---|
| *Continue Cups (Alternative 1) or Discontinue Cups (Alternative 2)* | | | | |
| | | | | |
| | | | | |
| | | | | |
| | | | | |
| | | | | |
| | | | | |
| | | | | |
| | | | | |
| | | | | |
| | | | | |
| | | | | |
| | | | | |

**B.** _____

_____

_____

_____

**EXERCISE 24-5**

**A.** _____

_____

_____

_____

_____

_____

_____

_____

_____

**B.** _____

_____

_____

_____

_____

_____

_____

_____

_____

_____

_____

_____

_____

_____

_____

_____

_____

**C.**

| | INVESTOR SERVICES (IN MILLIONS) | ADVISOR SERVICES (IN MILLIONS) | |
|---|---|---|---|
| | | | |
| | | | |
| | | | |
| | | | |

**EXERCISE 24-5, Concluded**

D. _____

_____

_____

_____

_____

_____

_____

_____

_____

**EXERCISE 24-6**

_____

_____

_____

_____

_____

_____

_____

_____

*Continue Children's Shoes (Alternative 1) or Discontinue Children's Shoes (Alternative 2)*

| | CONTINUE CHILDREN'S SHOES (ALTERNATIVE 1) | DISCONTINUE CHILDREN'S SHOES (ALTERNATIVE 2) | DIFFERENTIAL EFFECT ON INCOME (ALTERNATIVE 2) |
|---|---|---|---|
| | | | |
| | | | |
| | | | |
| | | | |
| | | | |
| | | | |
| | | | |
| | | | |
| | | | |
| | | | |

**EXERCISE 24-7**

A.

| Make Carrying Case (Alternative 1) or Buy Carrying Case (Alternative 2) | | | |
|---|---|---|---|
| | MAKE CARRYING CASE (ALTERNATIVE 1) | BUY CARRYING CASE (ALTERNATIVE 2) | DIFFERENTIAL EFFECT ON INCOME (ALTERNATIVE 2) |
| | | | |
| | | | |
| | | | |
| | | | |
| | | | |
| | | | |
| | | | |
| | | | |
| | | | |
| | | | |
| | | | |

B. _____

_____

_____

_____

_____

_____

_____

**EXERCISE 24-8**

A.

| | | *Lay Out Pages Internally (Alternative 1) or Purchase Layout Services (Alternative 2)* | |
|---|---|---|---|
| | LAY OUT PAGES INTERNALLY (ALTERNATIVE 1) | PURCHASE LAYOUT SERVICES (ALTERNATIVE 2) | DIFFERENTIAL EFFECT ON INCOME (ALTERNATIVE 2) |
| | | | |
| | | | |
| | | | |
| | | | |
| | | | |
| | | | |
| | | | |
| | | | |
| | | | |
| | | | |
| | | | |
| | | | |
| | | | |
| | | | |

B. _____

_____

_____

_____

_____

_____

_____

**EXERCISE 24-8, Concluded**

C. _____

_____

_____

_____

_____

_____

_____

_____

_____

_____

_____

**EXERCISE 24-9**

**A.**

| | Continue with Old Machine (Alternative 1) or Replace Old Machine (Alternative 2) | | |

| | CONTINUE WITH OLD MACHINE (ALTERNATIVE 1) | REPLACE OLD MACHINE (ALTERNATIVE 2) | DIFFERENTIAL EFFECT ON INCOME (ALTERNATIVE 2) |
|---|---|---|---|
| | | | |
| | | | |
| | | | |
| | | | |
| | | | |
| | | | |
| | | | |
| | | | |
| | | | |
| | | | |
| | | | |
| | | | |

**B.**

**EXERCISE 24-10**

**A.**

| | Continue with Old Machine (Alternative 1) or Replace Old Machine (Alternative 2) | | |
|---|---|---|---|
| | CONTINUE WITH OLD MACHINE (ALTERNATIVE 1) | REPLACE OLD MACHINE (ALTERNATIVE 2) | DIFFERENTIAL EFFECT ON INCOME (ALTERNATIVE 2) |
| | | | |
| | | | |
| | | | |
| | | | |
| | | | |
| | | | |
| | | | |
| | | | |
| | | | |
| | | | |
| | | | |
| | | | |
| | | | |
| | | | |

**B.** _____

_____

**C.** _____

_____

_____

_____

_____

_____

_____

_____

_____

**EXERCISE 24-11**

*Sell Rough-Cut (Alternative 1) or Process Further into Finished-Cut (Alternative 2)*

| | SELL ROUGH-CUT (ALTERNATIVE 1) | PROCESS FURTHER INTO FINISHED-CUT (ALTERNATIVE 2) | DIFFERENTIAL EFFECT ON INCOME (ALTERNATIVE 2) |
|---|---|---|---|
| | | | |
| | | | |
| | | | |
| | | | |
| | | | |
| | | | |
| | | | |

**EXERCISE 24-12**

A.

| Sell Regular Columbian (Alternative 1) or Process Further into Decaf Columbian (Alternative 2) | | | |
|---|---|---|---|
| | SELL REGULAR COLUMBIAN (ALTERNATIVE 1) | PROCESS FURTHER INTO DECAF COLUMBIAN (ALTERNATIVE 2) | DIFFERENTIAL EFFECT ON INCOME (ALTERNATIVE 2) |
| | | | |
| | | | |
| | | | |
| | | | |
| | | | |
| | | | |
| | | | |
| | | | |

B. _____

_____

_____

_____

_____

_____

_____

**EXERCISE 24-12, Concluded**

C. _____

_____

_____

_____

_____

_____

_____

_____

_____

_____

_____

_____

_____

_____

_____

_____

_____

_____

*Sell Regular Columbian (Alternative 1) or Process Further into Decaf Columbian (Alternative 2)*

|  | SELL REGULAR COLUMBIAN (ALTERNATIVE 1) | PROCESS FURTHER INTO DECAF COLUMBIAN (ALTERNATIVE 2) | DIFFERENTIAL EFFECT ON INCOME (ALTERNATIVE 2) |
|---|---|---|---|
|  |  |  |  |
|  |  |  |  |
|  |  |  |  |
|  |  |  |  |
|  |  |  |  |

**EXERCISE 24-13**

**A.**

| | Reject Order (Alternative 1) or Accept Order (Alternative 2) | | |
|---|---|---|---|

| | REJECT ORDER (ALTERNATIVE 1) | ACCEPT ORDER (ALTERNATIVE 2) | DIFFERENTIAL EFFECT ON INCOME (ALTERNATIVE 2) |
|---|---|---|---|
| | | | |
| | | | |
| | | | |
| | | | |
| | | | |
| | | | |
| | | | |

**B.** _____

_____

_____

_____

_____

_____

_____

_____

**C.** _____

_____

_____

**EXERCISE 24-14**

| | |
|---|---|
| | |
| | |
| | |
| | |

_____

_____

_____

_____

**EXERCISE 24-15**

**A.**

| | | | |
|---|---|---|---|
| *Reject Order (Alternative 1) or Accept Order (Alternative 2)* | | | |
| | REJECT ORDER (ALTERNATIVE 1) | ACCEPT ORDER (ALTERNATIVE 2) | DIFFERENTIAL EFFECT ON INCOME (ALTERNATIVE 2) |
| | | | |
| | | | |
| | | | |
| | | | |
| | | | |
| | | | |
| | | | |
| | | | |
| | | | |
| | | | |
| | | | |
| | | | |
| | | | |
| | | | |
| | | | |
| | | | |
| | | | |
| | | | |
| | | | |
| | | | |
| | | | |
| | | | |

**B.**

**EXERCISE 24-16**

A. _____

B. _____

_____

C. _____

_____

_____

_____

_____

_____

_____

_____

D.

_____

**EXERCISE 24-17**

A. _____

B. _____

_____

C. _____

_____

_____

_____

_____

_____

_____

_____

_____

_____

_____

_____

_____

**EXERCISE 24-17, Concluded**

**D.**

|  |  |  |
|---|---|---|
|  |  |  |
|  |  |  |
|  |  |  |
|  |  |  |

**EXERCISE 24-18**

**A.** _____

_____

_____

_____

_____

**B.** _____

_____

_____

_____

_____

_____

_____

_____

_____

_____

_____

_____

_____

**EXERCISE 24-19**

**A.** _____

_____

_____

_____

_____

_____

_____

_____

_____

_____

_____

_____

_____

_____

**B.** _____

**C.**

| | | |
|---|---|---|
| | | |
| | | |
| | | |
| | | |
| | | |
| | | |
| | | |
| | | |
| | | |
| | | |
| | | |
| | | |
| | | |
| | | |
| | | |

_____

_____

_____

**EXERCISE 24-20**

| | TYPE 5 | TYPE 10 | TYPE 20 | |
|---|---|---|---|---|
| | | | | |
| | | | | |
| | | | | |
| | | | | |
| | | | | |
| | | | | |
| | | | | |
| | | | | |
| | | | | |
| | | | | |
| | | | | |
| | | | | |
| | | | | |
| | | | | |
| | | | | |
| | | | | |
| | | | | |
| | | | | |
| | | | | |
| | | | | |
| | | | | |
| | | | | |

**EXERCISE 24-21**

**A.**

|  | LARGE | MEDIUM | SMALL | TOTAL |
|---|---|---|---|---|
|  |  |  |  |  |
|  |  |  |  |  |
|  |  |  |  |  |
|  |  |  |  |  |
|  |  |  |  |  |
|  |  |  |  |  |
|  |  |  |  |  |

**B.** _____

_____

|  | LARGE | MEDIUM | SMALL |
|---|---|---|---|
|  |  |  |  |
|  |  |  |  |
|  |  |  |  |
|  |  |  |  |
|  |  |  |  |
|  |  |  |  |

**APPENDIX EXERCISE 24-22**

A.

B.

C.

**APPENDIX EXERCISE 24-23**

A.

B.

C.

**PROBLEM 24-1 ___**

1.

_____
_____ *Operate* _____ *(Alternative 1) or Invest in Bonds (Alternative 2)*
_____

| | OPERATE _____ (ALTERNATIVE 1) | INVEST IN BONDS (ALTERNATIVE 2) | DIFFERENTIAL EFFECT ON INCOME (ALTERNATIVE 2) |
|---|---|---|---|
| | | | |
| | | | |
| | | | |
| | | | |
| | | | |
| | | | |
| | | | |
| | | | |
| | | | |
| | | | |
| | | | |
| | | | |

2. _____
   _____

3.

| | | |
|---|---|---|
| | | |
| | | |
| | | |
| | | |
| | | |
| | | |
| | | |
| | | |
| | | |
| | | |
| | | |
| | | |
| | | |

This Page Not Used.

**PROBLEM 24-2 ___**

1.

| | CONTINUE WITH OLD MACHINE (ALTERNATIVE 1) | REPLACE OLD MACHINE (ALTERNATIVE 2) | DIFFERENTIAL EFFECT ON INCOME (ALTERNATIVE 2) |
|---|---|---|---|
| Continue with Old Machine (Alternative 1) or Replace Old Machine (Alternative 2) | | | |
| | | | |
| | | | |
| | | | |
| | | | |
| | | | |
| | | | |
| | | | |
| | | | |
| | | | |
| | | | |
| | | | |

**PROBLEM 24-2 ___, Concluded**

2. _____

_____

_____

_____

_____

_____

_____

_____

_____

_____

_____

_____

_____

_____

_____

_____

_____

_____

_____

_____

_____

_____

_____

_____

**PROBLEM 24-3 ___**

1.

*Promote _____ (Alternative 1) or Promote _____ (Alternative 2)*

| | PROMOTE _____ (ALTERNATIVE 1) | PROMOTE _____ (ALTERNATIVE 2) | DIFFERENTIAL EFFECT ON INCOME (ALTERNATIVE 2) |
|---|---|---|---|
| | | | |
| | | | |
| | | | |
| | | | |
| | | | |
| | | | |
| | | | |
| | | | |
| | | | |
| | | | |
| | | | |
| | | | |
| | | | |
| | | | |
| | | | |
| | | | |
| | | | |

**PROBLEM 24-3 ___ , Concluded**

2. _____

_____

_____

_____

_____

_____

_____

_____

_____

_____

_____

_____

**PROBLEM 24-4 ___**

**1.**

_Sell _____ (Alternative 1) or Process Further into _____ (Alternative 2)_

| | SELL _____ (ALTERNATIVE 1) | PROCESS FURTHER INTO _____ (ALTERNATIVE 2) | DIFFERENTIAL EFFECT ON INCOME (ALTERNATIVE 2) | |
|---|---|---|---|---|
| | | | | |
| | | | | |
| | | | | |
| | | | | |
| | | | | |
| | | | | |
| | | | | |
| | | | | |
| | | | | |
| | | | | |
| | | | | |
| | | | | |
| | | | | |
| | | | | |

**2.** _____

_____

_____

_____

_____

_____

This Page Not Used.

**PROBLEM 24-5 ___**

1. _____

2. A.

| | | |
|---|---|---|
| | | |
| | | |
| | | |
| | | |
| | | |
| | | |

B. _____

C.

| | | |
|---|---|---|
| | | |
| | | |

**PROBLEM 24-5 ___, Continued**

3. (APPENDIX)

A.

B.

C.

**PROBLEM 24-5 ___ , Continued**

4. (APPENDIX)

A. _____
_____
_____

B. _____
_____
_____
_____
_____
_____
_____
_____
_____

C.

| | |
|---|---|
| | |
| | |
| | |

5. _____
_____
_____
_____
_____
_____
_____

**PROBLEM 24-5 ___ , Concluded**

6.  A.

| | Reject Order (Alternative 1) or Accept Order (Alternative 2) | | |
|---|---|---|---|
| | REJECT ORDER (ALTERNATIVE 1) | ACCEPT ORDER (ALTERNATIVE 2) | DIFFERENTIAL EFFECT ON INCOME (ALTERNATIVE 2) |
| | | | |
| | | | |
| | | | |
| | | | |
| | | | |
| | | | |
| | | | |
| | | | |
| | | | |
| | | | |
| | | | |

B. _____

_____

**PROBLEM 24-6 ____**

1.

| | | | |
|---|---|---|---|
| | | | |
| | | | |
| | | | |
| | | | |
| | | | |
| | | | |
| | | | |
| | | | |
| | | | |
| | | | |
| | | | |
| | | | |

**PROBLEM 24-6 ___, Concluded**

**2.**

|  |  |  |  |
|---|---|---|---|
|  |  |  |  |
|  |  |  |  |
|  |  |  |  |
|  |  |  |  |
|  |  |  |  |
|  |  |  |  |
|  |  |  |  |

Explanation:

_____

_____

_____

_____

_____

_____

_____

_____

_____

_____

_____

_____

_____

_____

_____

_____

_____

_____

**EXERCISE 25-1**

|  | 3D PRINTER | TRUCK |
|---|---|---|
|  |  |  |
|  |  |  |
|  |  |  |
|  |  |  |
|  |  |  |
|  |  |  |
|  |  |  |
|  |  |  |
|  |  |  |
|  |  |  |
|  |  |  |
|  |  |  |
|  |  |  |
|  |  |  |
|  |  |  |

**EXERCISE 25-2**

**EXERCISE 25-3**

_____

_____

_____

_____

_____

_____

_____

_____

_____

_____

_____

_____

_____

_____

_____

_____

_____

_____

_____

**EXERCISE 25-4**

|  | YEAR 1 | YEARS 2–9 | LAST YEAR |
|---|---|---|---|
|  |  |  |  |
|  |  |  |  |
|  |  |  |  |
|  |  |  |  |
|  |  |  |  |
|  |  |  |  |
|  |  |  |  |
|  |  |  |  |
|  |  |  |  |
|  |  |  |  |
|  |  |  |  |
|  |  |  |  |
|  |  |  |  |
|  |  |  |  |
|  |  |  |  |
|  |  |  |  |
|  |  |  |  |

## EXERCISE 25-5

_____
_____
_____

|  | NET CASH FLOW | CUMULATIVE NET CASH FLOWS |
|---|---|---|
|  |  |  |
|  |  |  |
|  |  |  |
|  |  |  |
|  |  |  |
|  |  |  |

## EXERCISE 25-6

A. _____
_____
_____
_____
_____
_____
_____

|  | LIQUID SOAP | | BODY LOTION | |
|---|---|---|---|---|
|  | NET CASH FLOW | CUMULATIVE NET CASH FLOWS | NET CASH FLOW | CUMULATIVE NET CASH FLOWS |
|  |  |  |  |  |
|  |  |  |  |  |
|  |  |  |  |  |
|  |  |  |  |  |
|  |  |  |  |  |
|  |  |  |  |  |
|  |  |  |  |  |

_____
_____

**EXERCISE 25-6, Concluded**

**B.** _____

_____

_____

_____

_____

_____

_____

_____

_____

_____

_____

_____

_____

_____

_____

**EXERCISE 25-7**

**A.**

| Year | Present Value of $1 at 15% | Net Cash Flow | Present Value of Net Cash Flow |
|:---:|:---:|:---:|:---:|
| 1 | | | |
| 2 | | | |
| 3 | | | |
| 4 | | | |
| Total ................................................ | | | |
| Amount to be invested ............................................ | | | |
| Net present value ............................................ | | | |

**B.** _____

_____

_____

**EXERCISE  25-8**

**A.**

|  | 20Y1 | 20Y2 | 20Y3 | 20Y4 | 20Y5 |
|---|---|---|---|---|---|
|  |  |  |  |  |  |
|  |  |  |  |  |  |
|  |  |  |  |  |  |
|  |  |  |  |  |  |
|  |  |  |  |  |  |
|  |  |  |  |  |  |
|  |  |  |  |  |  |
|  |  |  |  |  |  |
|  |  |  |  |  |  |

**B.**

| Year | Net Cash Flow [from part A.] | Present Value of $1 at 12% | Present Value of Net Cash Flow |
|---|---|---|---|
| 20Y1 |  |  |  |
| 20Y2 |  |  |  |
| 20Y3 |  |  |  |
| 20Y4 |  |  |  |
| 20Y5 |  |  |  |
| Total present value of cash flows.................................................................... |  |  |  |
| Investment in delivery truck....................................................................... |  |  |  |
| Net present value of delivery truck............................................................ |  |  |  |

**C.** _____

_____

_____

_____

_____

_____

**EXERCISE 25-9**

**A.**

|  | (IN MILLIONS) |  |
|---|---|---|
|  |  |  |
|  |  |  |
|  |  |  |
|  |  |  |
|  |  |  |

**B.**

|  | (IN MILLIONS, EXCEPT PRESENT VALUE FACTOR) |  |
|---|---|---|
|  |  |  |
|  |  |  |
|  |  |  |
|  |  |  |
|  |  |  |
|  |  |  |
|  |  |  |

**C.** _____

_____

_____

_____

_____

_____

**EXERCISE 25-10**

**A.**

| | | | | |
|---|---|---|---|---|
| | | | | |
| | | | | |
| | | | | |
| | | | | |
| | | | | |
| | | | | |
| | | | | |
| | | | | |
| | | | | |
| | | | | |
| | | | | |
| | | | | |
| | | | | |
| | | | | |
| | | | | |
| | | | | |
| | | | | |

**B.**

| | |
|---|---|
| | |
| | |
| | |
| | |
| | |
| | |

## EXERCISE 25-10, Concluded

**C.** _____

_____

_____

_____

**D.** _____

_____

_____

_____

_____

_____

_____

_____

## EXERCISE 25-11

**A.**

|  |  |  |
|---|---|---|
|  |  |  |
|  |  |  |
|  |  |  |
|  |  |  |
|  |  |  |

**B.**

|  |  |  |
|---|---|---|
|  |  |  |
|  |  |  |
|  |  |  |
|  |  |  |
|  |  |  |

**EXERCISE  25-12**

**A.** _____

_____

_____

_____

_____

_____

_____

_____

_____

_____

**B.** _____

_____

_____

_____

_____

**EXERCISE 25-13**

A. _____

_____

_____

_____

_____

_____

_____

Sewing Machine:

| | | |
|---|---|---|
| | | |
| | | |
| | | |
| | | |
| | | |
| | | |
| | | |
| | | |

Packing Machine:

| | | |
|---|---|---|
| | | |
| | | |
| | | |
| | | |
| | | |
| | | |
| | | |
| | | |

B. _____

_____

_____

_____

_____

_____

_____

_____

_____

**EXERCISE 25-13, Concluded**

C. _____

_____

_____

_____

_____

_____

_____

_____

_____

_____

_____

_____

_____

_____

_____

_____

_____

**EXERCISE 25-14**

A. _____

_____

_____

_____

_____

B. _____

_____

_____

C.

**EXERCISE 25-15**

**A.** _____

_____

_____

**B.** _____

_____

_____

_____

_____

**C.** _____

_____

_____

_____

_____

_____

_____

_____

_____

_____

_____

_____

_____

_____

_____

_____

_____

_____

_____

_____

_____

**EXERCISE 25-20**

_____

_____

_____

_____

_____

_____

_____

_____

_____

_____

_____

_____

**EXERCISE 25-21**

Processing Mill:

| Year | Present Value of $1 at 15% | Net Cash Flow | Present Value of Net Cash Flow |
|---|---|---|---|
| 1 | | | |
| 2 | | | |
| 3 | | | |
| 4 | | | |
| 4 (residual value) | | | |
| Total.................................... | | | |
| Amount to be invested................................... | | | |
| Net present value................................... | | | |

Electric Shovel:

| Year | Present Value of $1 at 15% | Net Cash Flow | Present Value of Net Cash Flow |
|---|---|---|---|
| 1 | | | |
| 2 | | | |
| 3 | | | |
| 4 | | | |
| Total.................................... | | | |
| Amount to be invested................................... | | | |
| Net present value................................... | | | |

Conclusion with explanation:

_____

_____

_____

_____

_____

_____

_____

_____

**EXERCISE 25-22**

**A.** Blending Equipment:

| | | | |
|---|---|---|---|
| | | | |
| | | | |
| | | | |
| | | | |
| | | | |
| | | | |
| | | | |
| | | | |
| | | | |
| | | | |
| | | | |
| | | | |
| | | | |
| | | | |
| | | | |
| | | | |
| | | | |

Computer System:

| | | | |
|---|---|---|---|
| | | | |
| | | | |
| | | | |
| | | | |
| | | | |
| | | | |

**B.** _____

_____

_____

_____

_____

_____

_____

_____

_____

_____

_____

**This Page Not Used.**

**PROBLEM 25-1 ___**

1. A. _____

   _____

   _____

   _____

   _____

   _____

   B.

| Year | Present Value of $1 at _____% | Net Cash Flow | | Present Value of Net Cash Flow | |
|------|------------------------------|---------------|--|--------------------------------|--|
|      |                              | Project: _____ | Project: _____ | Project: _____ | Project: _____ |
| 1    |                              |               |  |                                |  |
| 2    |                              |               |  |                                |  |
| 3    |                              |               |  |                                |  |
| 4    |                              |               |  |                                |  |
| 5    |                              |               |  |                                |  |
| Total............................ |        |               |  |                                |  |
| Amount to be invested................................................. |        |        |  |  |  |
| Net present value .................................................. |        |        |  |  |  |

2. _____

   _____

   _____

   _____

   _____

   _____

   _____

   _____

   _____

   _____

   _____

   _____

   _____

   _____

450

**This Page Not Used.**

**PROBLEM 25-2 ___**

**1. A.**

| Year | Net Cash Flow | Cumulative Net Cash Flow |
|---|---|---|
|  |  |  |
|  |  |  |
|  |  |  |

| Year | Net Cash Flow | Cumulative Net Cash Flow |
|---|---|---|
|  |  |  |
|  |  |  |
|  |  |  |

**B.**

| Year | Present Value of $1 at _____% | Net Cash Flow Project (Product): _____ | Net Cash Flow Project (Product): _____ | Present Value of Net Cash Flow Project (Product): _____ | Present Value of Net Cash Flow Project (Product): _____ |
|---|---|---|---|---|---|
| 1 |  |  |  |  |  |
| 2 |  |  |  |  |  |
| 3 |  |  |  |  |  |
| 4 |  |  |  |  |  |
| 5 |  |  |  |  |  |
| Total |  |  |  |  |  |
| Amount to be invested |  |  |  |  |  |
| Net present value |  |  |  |  |  |

**PROBLEM 25-2 ___, Concluded**

2. _____

_____

_____

_____

_____

_____

_____

_____

_____

_____

_____

_____

_____

_____

_____

_____

_____

_____

**PROBLEM 25-3 ___**

**1.** Proposal (Project): _____

| Year | Present Value of $1 at _____% | Net Cash Flow | Present Value of Net Cash Flow |
|------|------|------|------|
| 1 | | | |
| 2 | | | |
| 3 | | | |
| Total.................................................... | | | |
| Amount to be invested................................................ | | | |
| Net present value ................................................ | | | |

Proposal (Project): _____

| Year | Present Value of $1 at _____% | Net Cash Flow | Present Value of Net Cash Flow |
|------|------|------|------|
| 1 | | | |
| 2 | | | |
| 3 | | | |
| Total.................................................... | | | |
| Amount to be invested................................................ | | | |
| Net present value ................................................ | | | |

Proposal (Project): _____

| Year | Present Value of $1 at _____% | Net Cash Flow | Present Value of Net Cash Flow |
|------|------|------|------|
| 1 | | | |
| 2 | | | |
| 3 | | | |
| Total.................................................... | | | |
| Amount to be invested................................................ | | | |
| Net present value ................................................ | | | |

**PROBLEM 25-3 ___, Concluded**

**2.** _____

_____

_____

_____

_____

_____

_____

_____

_____

_____

_____

**3.** _____

_____

_____

_____

_____

_____

_____

_____

_____

_____

_____

**PROBLEM 25-4 ___**

1. **A.** Project: _____

| | | |
|---|---|---|
| | | |
| | | |
| | | |
| | | |
| | | |
| | | |
| | | |

Project: _____

| | | |
|---|---|---|
| | | |
| | | |
| | | |
| | | |
| | | |
| | | |
| | | |

**B.** _____

_____

_____

_____

_____

_____

_____

_____

_____

**PROBLEM 25-4 ___, Concluded**

2.  A. _____

_____

_____

_____

_____

_____

_____

_____

_____

_____

    B. _____

_____

_____

_____

_____

3. _____

_____

_____

_____

_____

_____

_____

_____

_____

_____

_____

_____

_____

_____

_____

_____

_____

**PROBLEM 25-5 ___**

**1.** Project (Site): _____

| | |
|---|---|
| | |
| | |
| | |
| | |
| | |
| | |
| | |

Project (Site): _____

| | |
|---|---|
| | |
| | |
| | |
| | |
| | |
| | |

**2.**

| Year | Present Value of $1 at _____% | Net Cash Flow | | Present Value of Net Cash Flow | |
|---|---|---|---|---|---|
| | | Project (Site): _____ | Project (Site): _____ | Project (Site): _____ | Project (Site): _____ |
| 1 | | | | | |
| 2 | | | | | |
| 3 | | | | | |
| 4 | | | | | |
| 4 (residual value) | | | | | |
| Total ............................ | | | | | |
| Amount to be invested ............................................. | | | | | |
| Net present value................................................ | | | | | |

**PROBLEM 25-5 ___, Concluded**

3. _____

_____

_____

_____

_____

_____

_____

_____

_____

_____

_____

_____

_____

_____

_____

_____

_____

_____

**PROBLEM  25-6 ___**

**1.** Proposal A:

| Year | Net Cash Flow | Cumulative Net Cash Flows |
|------|---------------|---------------------------|
|      |               |                           |
|      |               |                           |
|      |               |                           |
|      |               |                           |
|      |               |                           |

Proposal B:

| Year | Net Cash Flow | Cumulative Net Cash Flows |
|------|---------------|---------------------------|
|      |               |                           |
|      |               |                           |
|      |               |                           |
|      |               |                           |
|      |               |                           |

Proposal C:

| Year | Net Cash Flow | Cumulative Net Cash Flows |
|------|---------------|---------------------------|
|      |               |                           |
|      |               |                           |
|      |               |                           |
|      |               |                           |
|      |               |                           |

Proposal D:

| Year | Net Cash Flow | Cumulative Net Cash Flows |
|------|---------------|---------------------------|
|      |               |                           |
|      |               |                           |
|      |               |                           |
|      |               |                           |
|      |               |                           |

**PROBLEM  25-6 ____ ,  Continued**

2.  Proposal A: _____

_____

_____

_____

_____

_____

Proposal B: _____

_____

_____

_____

_____

_____

Proposal C: _____

_____

_____

_____

_____

_____

Proposal D: _____

_____

_____

_____

_____

_____

**PROBLEM 25-6 ___,  Continued**

**3.**

| Proposal | Cash Payback Period | Average Rate of Return | Accept for Further Analysis | Reject |
|---|---|---|---|---|
| A | | | | |
| B | | | | |
| C | | | | |
| D | | | | |

**4.** Proposal ___:

| Year | Present Value of $1 at _____% | Net Cash Flow | Present Value of Net Cash Flow |
|---|---|---|---|
| 1 | | | |
| 2 | | | |
| 3 | | | |
| 4 | | | |
| 5 | | | |
| Total............................................................ | | | |
| Amount to be invested.................................................... | | | |
| Net present value ........................................................ | | | |

Proposal ___:

| Year | Present Value of $1 at _____% | Net Cash Flow | Present Value of Net Cash Flow |
|---|---|---|---|
| 1 | | | |
| 2 | | | |
| 3 | | | |
| 4 | | | |
| 5 | | | |
| Total............................................................ | | | |
| Amount to be invested.................................................... | | | |
| Net present value ........................................................ | | | |

**PROBLEM 25-6 ___, Concluded**

5. _____

_____

_____

_____

_____

_____

_____

_____

6. _____

_____

_____

_____

7. _____

_____

_____

_____

_____

8. _____

_____

_____

_____

_____

_____

_____

**EXERCISE 26-1**

_____
_____
_____
_____
_____
_____
_____
_____
_____
_____
_____
_____
_____
_____
_____
_____
_____
_____
_____
_____
_____
_____
_____

**EXERCISE 26-2**

**EXERCISE  26-3**

**EXERCISE 26-4**

_____

_____

_____

_____

_____

_____

_____

_____

_____

_____

_____

_____

_____

**EXERCISE 26-5**

A. _____

_____

_____

_____

_____

_____

_____

_____

_____

_____

_____

_____

_____

_____

**EXERCISE 26-5, Concluded**

**B.** _____

_____

_____

_____

_____

_____

_____

_____

_____

_____

_____

_____

_____

_____

_____

_____

_____

_____

_____

_____

_____

_____

_____

_____

_____

**C.**

| | |
|---|---|
| | |
| | |
| | |
| | |
| | |
| | |

**EXERCISE 26-6**

*Traditional Philosophy*

| | VALUE-ADDED TIME | NON-VALUE-ADDED TIME | TOTAL TIME | |
|---|---|---|---|---|
| | | | | |
| | | | | |
| | | | | |
| | | | | |
| | | | | |
| | | | | |
| | | | | |
| | | | | |
| | | | | |
| | | | | |
| | | | | |
| | | | | |
| | | | | |
| | | | | |

## EXERCISE 26-6, Concluded

*Lean Manufacturing Philosophy*

| | VALUE-ADDED TIME | NON-VALUE-ADDED TIME | TOTAL TIME |
|---|---|---|---|
| | | | |
| | | | |
| | | | |
| | | | |
| | | | |
| | | | |
| | | | |
| | | | |
| | | | |
| | | | |
| | | | |
| | | | |
| | | | |
| | | | |
| | | | |
| | | | |

**EXERCISE 26-7**

*Present Approach*

| | VALUE-ADDED TIME | NON-VALUE-ADDED TIME | TOTAL TIME | |
|---|---|---|---|---|
| | | | | |
| | | | | |
| | | | | |
| | | | | |
| | | | | |
| | | | | |
| | | | | |
| | | | | |
| | | | | |
| | | | | |
| | | | | |
| | | | | |
| | | | | |
| | | | | |
| | | | | |
| | | | | |
| | | | | |
| | | | | |
| | | | | |
| | | | | |
| | | | | |
| | | | | |

_____

_____

_____

_____

_____

**EXERCISE 26-7, Concluded**

*Proposed Lean Approach*

| | VALUE-ADDED TIME | NON-VALUE-ADDED TIME | TOTAL TIME |
|---|---|---|---|
| | | | |
| | | | |
| | | | |
| | | | |
| | | | |
| | | | |
| | | | |
| | | | |
| | | | |
| | | | |
| | | | |
| | | | |
| | | | |
| | | | |
| | | | |
| | | | |
| | | | |
| | | | |
| | | | |
| | | | |

**EXERCISE 26-8**

A. _____

_____

_____

_____

_____

_____

_____

_____

_____

_____

_____

_____

_____

_____

B. _____

_____

_____

_____

_____

_____

_____

_____

_____

_____

_____

_____

_____

_____

**EXERCISE 26-8, Concluded**

C. _____

_____

_____

_____

_____

_____

_____

_____

_____

_____

_____

_____

_____

_____

**EXERCISE 26-9**

**EXERCISE 26-10**

A. _____

_____

_____

_____

_____

_____

_____

_____

_____

_____

_____

_____

_____

_____

**EXERCISE 26-10, Concluded**

B. _____

_____

_____

_____

_____

_____

_____

_____

_____

_____

_____

_____

_____

_____

_____

_____

_____

_____

_____

_____

_____

_____

_____

_____

_____

_____

_____

_____

_____

_____

_____

**EXERCISE 26-11**

**EXERCISE 26-12**

A. _____

_____

_____

_____

_____

B. _____

_____

_____

_____

_____

_____

_____

**EXERCISE 26-12, Concluded**

**C. (1) through (4)**

## JOURNAL

| | DATE | | DESCRIPTION | POST. REF. | DEBIT | CREDIT | |
|---|---|---|---|---|---|---|---|
| 1 | | | | | | | 1 |
| 2 | | | | | | | 2 |
| 3 | | | | | | | 3 |
| 4 | | | | | | | 4 |
| 5 | | | | | | | 5 |
| 6 | | | | | | | 6 |
| 7 | | | | | | | 7 |
| 8 | | | | | | | 8 |
| 9 | | | | | | | 9 |
| 10 | | | | | | | 10 |
| 11 | | | | | | | 11 |
| 12 | | | | | | | 12 |
| 13 | | | | | | | 13 |
| 14 | | | | | | | 14 |
| 15 | | | | | | | 15 |
| 16 | | | | | | | 16 |
| 17 | | | | | | | 17 |
| 18 | | | | | | | 18 |
| 19 | | | | | | | 19 |
| 20 | | | | | | | 20 |
| 21 | | | | | | | 21 |
| 22 | | | | | | | 22 |
| 23 | | | | | | | 23 |
| 24 | | | | | | | 24 |
| 25 | | | | | | | 25 |
| 26 | | | | | | | 26 |
| 27 | | | | | | | 27 |
| 28 | | | | | | | 28 |

**EXERCISE 26-13**

A. _____

_____

_____

_____

_____

B. _____

_____

_____

_____

_____

_____

_____

**EXERCISE 26-13, Concluded**

**C. (1) through (4)**

**JOURNAL**                                    PAGE

| | DATE | DESCRIPTION | POST. REF. | DEBIT | CREDIT | |
|---|---|---|---|---|---|---|
| 1 | | | | | | 1 |
| 2 | | | | | | 2 |
| 3 | | | | | | 3 |
| 4 | | | | | | 4 |
| 5 | | | | | | 5 |
| 6 | | | | | | 6 |
| 7 | | | | | | 7 |
| 8 | | | | | | 8 |
| 9 | | | | | | 9 |
| 10 | | | | | | 10 |
| 11 | | | | | | 11 |
| 12 | | | | | | 12 |
| 13 | | | | | | 13 |
| 14 | | | | | | 14 |
| 15 | | | | | | 15 |
| 16 | | | | | | 16 |
| 17 | | | | | | 17 |
| 18 | | | | | | 18 |
| 19 | | | | | | 19 |
| 20 | | | | | | 20 |
| 21 | | | | | | 21 |
| 22 | | | | | | 22 |
| 23 | | | | | | 23 |
| 24 | | | | | | 24 |
| 25 | | | | | | 25 |
| 26 | | | | | | 26 |
| 27 | | | | | | 27 |
| 28 | | | | | | 28 |

**EXERCISE 26-14**

**A.  (1) through (4)**

**JOURNAL**

PAGE

| | DATE | DESCRIPTION | POST. REF. | DEBIT | CREDIT | |
|---|---|---|---|---|---|---|
| 1 | | | | | | 1 |
| 2 | | | | | | 2 |
| 3 | | | | | | 3 |
| 4 | | | | | | 4 |
| 5 | | | | | | 5 |
| 6 | | | | | | 6 |
| 7 | | | | | | 7 |
| 8 | | | | | | 8 |
| 9 | | | | | | 9 |
| 10 | | | | | | 10 |
| 11 | | | | | | 11 |
| 12 | | | | | | 12 |
| 13 | | | | | | 13 |
| 14 | | | | | | 14 |
| 15 | | | | | | 15 |
| 16 | | | | | | 16 |
| 17 | | | | | | 17 |
| 18 | | | | | | 18 |
| 19 | | | | | | 19 |
| 20 | | | | | | 20 |
| 21 | | | | | | 21 |
| 22 | | | | | | 22 |
| 23 | | | | | | 23 |
| 24 | | | | | | 24 |
| 25 | | | | | | 25 |
| 26 | | | | | | 26 |
| 27 | | | | | | 27 |
| 28 | | | | | | 28 |

**EXERCISE 26-14, Concluded**

**B.**

| | |
|---|---|
| | |
| | |
| | |
| | |

Supporting calculations:

| | |
|---|---|
| | |
| | |
| | |
| | |

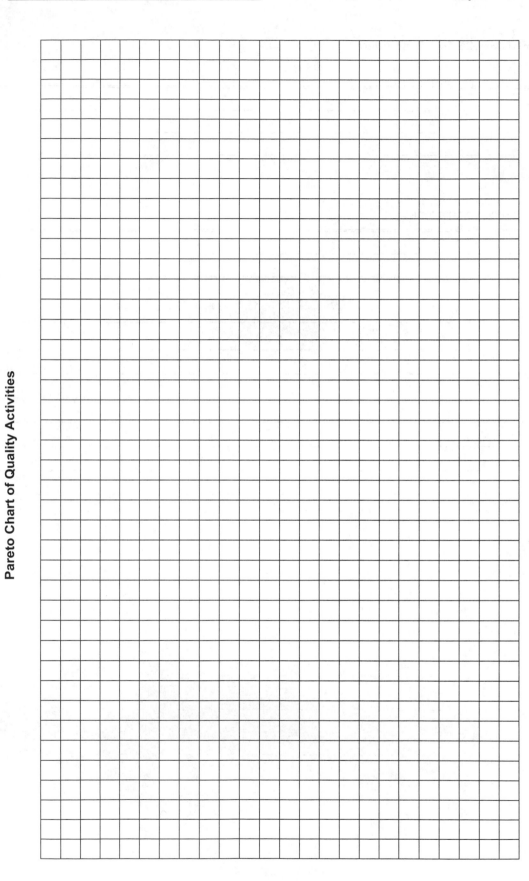

**Pareto Chart of Quality Activities**

Dollars

**EXERCISE 26-15**

**EXERCISE 26-16**

**A.**

| Quality Activities | Activity Cost | Quality Cost Classification |
|---|---|---|
| Correct shipment errors ............................ | $  150,000 | |
| Disposing of scrap ................................... | 95,000 | |
| Emergency equipment maintenance ........ | 125,000 | |
| Employee training ................................... | 50,000 | |
| Final inspection ...................................... | 80,000 | |
| Inspecting incoming materials................... | 60,000 | |
| Preventive equipment maintenance ......... | 40,000 | |
| Processing customer returns ................... | 90,000 | |
| Scrap reporting........................................ | 45,000 | |
| Supplier development .............................. | 15,000 | |
| Warranty claims ...................................... | 250,000 | |
| Total................................................ | $1,000,000 | |

**B.**

*Cost of Quality Report*

| QUALITY COST CLASSIFICATION | COST SUMMARY | | |
|---|---|---|---|
| | QUALITY COST | PERCENT OF TOTAL QUALITY COST | PERCENT OF TOTAL SALES |
| | | | |
| | | | |
| | | | |
| | | | |
| | | | |
| | | | |
| | | | |

**EXERCISE 26-16, Concluded**

C. _____

_____

_____

_____

_____

_____

_____

_____

_____

_____

_____

EXERCISE 26-17

**Pareto Chart of Quality Activities**

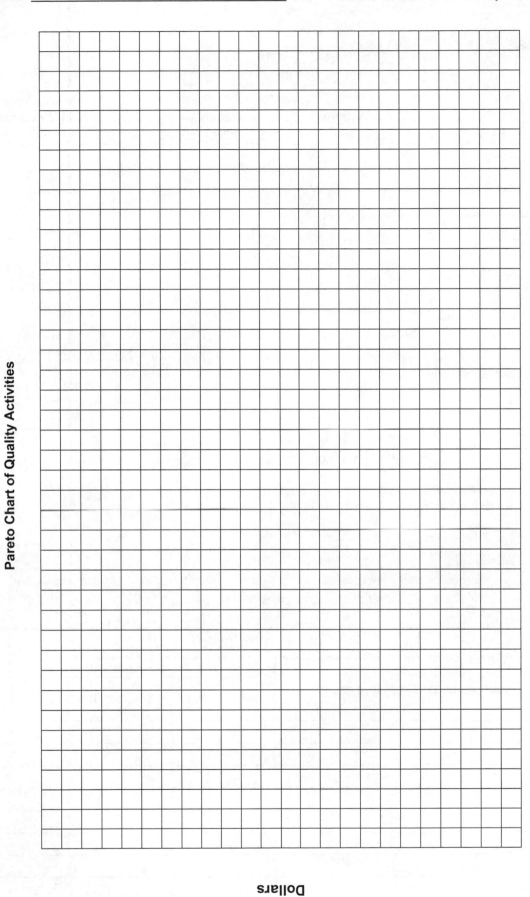

Dollars

**EXERCISE  26-18**

A.

| Quality Activities | Activity Cost | Quality Cost Classification | Value-Added/ Non-Value Added Classification |
|---|---|---|---|
| Billing error correction ....... | $ 60,000 | | |
| Cable signal testing........... | 140,000 | | |
| Reinstalling service (installed incorrectly the first time) ........................ | 40,000 | | |
| Repairing satellite equipment ...................... | 50,000 | | |
| Repairing underground cable connections to the customer ................... | 25,000 | | |
| Replacing old technology cable with higher quality cable ................... | 175,000 | | |
| Replacing old technology signal switches with higher quality switches.... | 150,000 | | |
| Responding to customer home repair requests ...... | 30,000 | | |
| Training employees........... | 80,000 | | |
| Total............................ | $750,000 | | |

B.

**Cost of Quality Report**

| QUALITY COST CLASSIFICATION | COST SUMMARY | | |
|---|---|---|---|
| | QUALITY COST | PERCENT OF TOTAL QUALITY COST | PERCENT OF TOTAL SALES |
| | | | |
| | | | |
| | | | |
| | | | |
| | | | |
| | | | |
| | | | |
| | | | |

**EXERCISE 26-18, Concluded**

**C.**

| | | |
|---|---|---|
| *Value-Added/Non-Value-Added Activity Analysis* | | |
| CATEGORY | AMOUNT | PERCENT |
| | | |
| | | |
| | | |
| | | |

**D.** _____

_____

_____

_____

_____

_____

_____

_____

_____

_____

_____

_____

**EXERCISE 26-19**

**A.** _____

_____

_____

_____

_____

_____

_____

**B.** _____

_____

_____

_____

_____

_____

_____

_____

_____

|  |  |  |
|---|---|---|
|  |  |  |
|  |  |  |
|  |  |  |
|  |  |  |
|  |  |  |

Calculations:

_____

_____

_____

_____

_____

_____

_____

**EXERCISE 26-19, Concluded**

C. _____

_____

_____

_____

_____

_____

_____

_____

_____

_____

_____

_____

_____

_____

_____

_____

_____

_____

_____

_____

_____

_____

_____

**EXERCISE 26-20**

**A.**

| ACTIVITY | COST | PERCENT OF TOTAL PROCESS |
|---|---|---|
|  |  |  |
|  |  |  |
|  |  |  |
|  |  |  |
|  |  |  |
|  |  |  |

**B.** _____

_____

_____

**C.**

| ACTIVITY | ACTIVITY COST PRIOR TO IMPROVEMENT | ACTIVITY COST AFTER IMPROVEMENT | ACTIVITY COST SAVINGS (COST) |
|---|---|---|---|
|  |  |  |  |
|  |  |  |  |
|  |  |  |  |
|  |  |  |  |
|  |  |  |  |
|  |  |  |  |
|  |  |  |  |

**D.** _____

_____

_____

**EXERCISE 26-21**

**A.**

| ACTIVITY | COST | PERCENT OF TOTAL PROCESS | |
|---|---|---|---|
| | | | |
| | | | |
| | | | |
| | | | |
| | | | |
| | | | |
| | | | |
| | | | |
| | | | |
| | | | |
| | | | |
| | | | |
| | | | |
| | | | |

**B.** _____

_____

_____

**EXERCISE 26-21, Concluded**

**C.**

| ACTIVITY | ACTIVITY COST PRIOR TO IMPROVEMENT | ACTIVITY COST AFTER IMPROVEMENT | ACTIVITY COST SAVINGS | |
|---|---|---|---|---|
| | | | | |
| | | | | |
| | | | | |
| | | | | |
| | | | | |
| | | | | |
| | | | | |
| | | | | |
| | | | | |
| | | | | |
| | | | | |
| | | | | |
| | | | | |
| | | | | |
| | | | | |
| | | | | |
| | | | | |
| | | | | |

**D.** _____

_____

_____

**PROBLEM 26-1 ___**

1. _____

_____

_____

_____

_____

_____

_____

_____

_____

_____

_____

_____

_____

_____

_____

_____

_____

_____

_____

_____

_____

_____

**PROBLEM 26-1 ___, Continued**

2. _____

_____

_____

_____

_____

_____

_____

_____

_____

_____

_____

_____

_____

_____

_____

_____

_____

_____

_____

_____

_____

_____

_____

**PROBLEM 26-1 ___ , Concluded**

3. _____

498

**This Page Not Used.**

**PROBLEM 26-2 ___**

**1.** Value-added time:

| | | |
|---|---|---|
| | | |
| | | |
| | | |
| | | |
| | | |
| | | |

Non-value-added time:

| | | |
|---|---|---|
| | | |
| | | |
| | | |
| | | |
| | | |
| | | |
| | | |
| | | |
| | | |
| | | |
| | | |
| | | |
| | | |
| | | |
| | | |
| | | |
| | | |

Value-added ratio:

_____

_____

_____

_____

_____

**PROBLEM 26-2 ___ , Concluded**

2. _____

_____

_____

_____

_____

_____

_____

_____

_____

_____

_____

_____

_____

_____

_____

_____

_____

_____

**PROBLEM 26-3 ___**

1. _____

_____

_____

_____

_____

2. _____

_____

_____

_____

_____

**PROBLEM 26-3 ___ , Continued**

3. (A) through (D)

## JOURNAL

PAGE

| | DATE | | DESCRIPTION | POST. REF. | DEBIT | CREDIT | |
|---|---|---|---|---|---|---|---|
| 1 | | | | | | | 1 |
| 2 | | | | | | | 2 |
| 3 | | | | | | | 3 |
| 4 | | | | | | | 4 |
| 5 | | | | | | | 5 |
| 6 | | | | | | | 6 |
| 7 | | | | | | | 7 |
| 8 | | | | | | | 8 |
| 9 | | | | | | | 9 |
| 10 | | | | | | | 10 |
| 11 | | | | | | | 11 |
| 12 | | | | | | | 12 |
| 13 | | | | | | | 13 |
| 14 | | | | | | | 14 |
| 15 | | | | | | | 15 |
| 16 | | | | | | | 16 |
| 17 | | | | | | | 17 |
| 18 | | | | | | | 18 |
| 19 | | | | | | | 19 |
| 20 | | | | | | | 20 |
| 21 | | | | | | | 21 |
| 22 | | | | | | | 22 |
| 23 | | | | | | | 23 |
| 24 | | | | | | | 24 |
| 25 | | | | | | | 25 |
| 26 | | | | | | | 26 |
| 27 | | | | | | | 27 |
| 28 | | | | | | | 28 |

**PROBLEM 26-3 \_\_\_, Concluded**

4. _____

_____

_____

_____

_____

_____

5. _____

_____

_____

_____

_____

_____

_____

_____

_____

_____

_____

_____

_____

_____

_____

_____

_____

This Page Not Used.

PROBLEM 26-4 _____

1.

**Pareto Chart of Quality Activities**

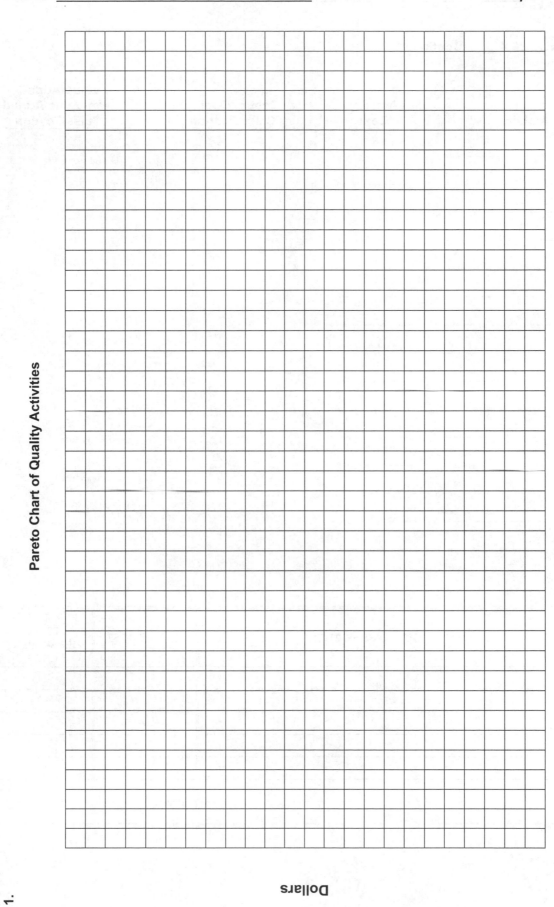

Dollars

**PROBLEM 26-4 ___, Continued**

2.

| Activity | Activity Cost | Cost of Quality Classification | Value-Added/ Non-Value Added Classification |
|---|---|---|---|
| _____ | _____ | | |
| _____ | _____ | | |
| _____ | _____ | | |
| _____ | _____ | | |
| _____ | _____ | | |
| _____ | _____ | | |
| _____ | _____ | | |
| _____ | _____ | | |
| _____ | _____ | | |
| _____ | _____ | | |
| _____ | _____ | | |
| _____ | _____ | | |
| _____ | _____ | | |
| _____ | _____ | | |

3.

| QUALITY COST CLASSIFICATION | ACTIVITY COST | PERCENT OF TOTAL DEPARTMENT COST |
|---|---|---|
| | | |
| | | |
| | | |
| | | |
| | | |
| | | |
| | | |
| | | |

**PROBLEM 26-4 ___ , Concluded**

4.

| | ACTIVITY COST | PERCENT OF TOTAL DEPARTMENT COST | |
|---|---|---|---|
| | | | |
| | | | |
| | | | |
| | | | |

5. _____

_____

_____

_____

_____

_____

_____

_____

_____

_____

_____

This Page Not Used.